Life: A Story of Believing

Anna-Louise Bates

Independently published by Anna-Louise Bates

PB ISBN: 9798336609608

Copyright © 2024 by Anna-Louise Bates

All rights reserved.

No portion of this book may be reproduced in any form without written permission from the publisher or author, except as permitted by U.K. copyright law.

"A powerful story of strength, love, and hope coming out of unimaginable loss and profound sadness. An extraordinary book."
Mark Lewis Jones (actor)

***

"Her journey is one that will touch your heart."
Ruth Jones (author)

***

"It really is quite the most remarkable book. The book is full of heart, which beats on every page. It is a journey of courage, hope, determination, life, and death. You will feel truly humbled reading her journey."
Jane Matthews – mother of a liver recipient

***

"It is one of those books that I found life-changing. I was captivated."
Lucy Beddall

***

"Anna's story highlights the complex psychological effects resulting from trauma and loss, yet also how it is possible to navigate these to experience post-traumatic growth and find further meaning in life. This book demonstrates Anna's heartfelt courage and love and how the deepest resilience of the human spirit can be realised, often through the most painful of experiences."

Dr Danielle Dummett (Clinical Psychologist)

***

"Anna is one brave woman. Her story is raw and would have completely finished off so many others. Instead, with courage, she has turned a shocking tragedy, led by her own selfless example, into an organization that literally saves lives. Please read the book and await the movie."

Mike Young (Emmy and BAFTA Award-winning animator and creator of SuperTed)

Acknowledgements

To Zach for encouraging and supporting me through the entire process of writing the book.

To Elizabeth for continuing to believe in me and for being emotionally intelligent enough to ground me and to allow me to feel her vision.

To Mum and Dad for continuing to hold my hands and being there not only as parents, but as my best friends who never tire of hearing about the charity - and for riding this constant rollercoaster of life by my side.

To Grandma, Mum, second mum Vivie, Bridget, and the other strong female role models that I've been blessed to have within my family, and who continue to inspire me.

To my 'fairy' godmother, Elizabeth's godmother and bff Ju Ju, who makes us smile even when wiping away the tears.

Father Irving, more than just my priest; despite what we have been through with Fraser, both together and separately, you continue to guide and support me in so many different ways.

To all my friends and family at St Martins for continuing to keep the faith.

To my brother and sister, not only for their love and performance in their allocated roles in their grief, but for putting up with every hare-brained idea from their annoying little sister!

To Ruth Jones and Mark Lewis Jones, for giving up their time to listen to me; for supporting me emotionally and for supporting the work of the charity.

To all of my trustees, ambassadors, and anyone who has taken time to assist in any way to further the objectives.

To Zoe and Ryan for allowing me so sensitively to have that bond with Roman; and to Roman and his siblings for the cwtchs and sheer unconditional love.

To Linda for listening and understanding and finding the right words for me and Patric for making this publication possible and telling me that my voice was not to be silenced.

Finally, to Mike; for not just providing me with the most amazing tribute to my boys, but for being mine and Elizabeth's role model and friend; together with Liz, you make us feel part of your family.

fidem vita fateri

Contents

Preface   1

1. Early Days   3
2. Mr Schmooze   13
3. Fraser   26
4. Another Pregnancy   37
5. Elizabeth and Fraser   45
6. The Party   58
7. The Incident   65
8. Fraser Passes   76
9. A Shrine   88
10. Aftermath   96
11. Believe is Born   106
12. Plans   115
13. A Funeral   123

14.	GMTV	133
15.	A Court Case	144
16.	Pride of Britain And Joan Collins	158
17.	PTSD And A Hole In My Heart	168
18.	Games And A Search For A Voice	176
19.	Letters	186
20.	Snow And A Message	193
21.	Zach	202
22.	A Marriage	213
23.	A Shared Heart	225
24.	The Wall	239
25.	Behind The Mask	251
26.	Distractions	262
27.	Looking Forward	275
28.	A Reflection	285
29.	Epilogue	295

Preface

You know my story. You've read the back of this book, or you've seen me and my boys in the media, and you know.

But actually, you don't know at all, because even *I* don't know all of my story – I can't even remember how every bit of it transpired and I certainly don't know how it will end. All that is certain is that the thing that should never happen to anyone happened to me.

We have all been through grief, or we will. Death is part of life, and there isn't a single person in this world who won't have to deal with the repercussions of losing someone they love. And yet, despite that, we don't deal terribly well with loss in our culture. We deflect and minimise, we mumble our condolences and shuffle away as the bereaved person deals with the enormity, the unimaginable magnitude, of what has been taken from them.

There's an army of us out there.

This is the story of one member of that army; of how I became the woman I am today, of how I loved and lost . . . and continued to love. It's the story of having my husband and my son ripped from me, and of how I, with my daughter, fought to survive. It's the story of how grief continues to live alongside your new life. It's the story of how you get through every second of every day with your heart breaking, but also the fight to do something to make a difference in memory of those who have gone.

It's the story of my Mr Wonderful and my Fraser Bear.

It's a story of believing.

Chapter One

Early Days

The summer of 1976 still lingers in the memories of so many people in the UK.

The days were swelteringly hot. It felt like the evenings went on forever and everyone just seemed to be happier. Or so I'm told. Having been born in the February, I was a newborn in a pram, sitting in the garden for most of that long, hot summer. I'm not one of those with the halcyon memories!

I catch the sun even now as I was used to it from such an early age. It's not your typical Cardiff-born look. I had an older brother and sister waiting for me when I came into the world - Martin who was seven, and Bridget who was five. They were fantastic siblings who always made me feel welcome, to the extent that I was almost the toy that they fought over!

At that point, everyone thought my mum was an only child, and only Dad's family had siblings, so I had cousins on that side. I was the youngest of everyone and I've always been the baby of the family. As I got older, I would joke that I was the mistake, but they always said, 'No, you were the compromise!' Dad would have gone on, but Mum said she only wanted one more. I was never made to feel like a baby who wasn't wanted though. My childhood was always lovely, warm, and nurturing.

Mum and Dad were brilliant marital role models. They had met at a dance at the Paget Rooms in Penarth, a historic theatre where plenty of young couples found their future husbands and wives in those days. Mum had been brought up in a vicarage where Grandma Dorothy was the housekeeper, and Mum was warned off Dad by her friends a little bit. He was a bit of a heartthrob, a lothario with a reputation for being 'fast.' A good girl like Mum (or so we thought) who had been brought up in a religious setting, couldn't possibly be associated with such a character! She ignored everyone and they were engaged within six months and married the next year.

Dad was faced with a fiancée whose nights were curtailed by curfews and he didn't just have to face my grandmother, but the many Fathers who were very suspicious of this cheeky character hanging around young Mary Le-Loux. All of those barriers and warnings became part of the story of their enduring and unstoppable love though. On one occasion, Mum was late for her curfew and Dad had to break into the vicarage through the side window to let her in without anyone knowing.

They both had such interesting lives before they got married and I think that being their own people, really helped them to become a strong couple. Dad was born at the beginning of WW2 and started as a salesman when he was only sixteen. He travelled the world with friends and his business, whereas my mum went to Paris when she was seventeen, to become an au pair. The family there treated her poorly and on her day off, she had so little money that she just sat on the Metro, going round and round all day. All three of us were brought up on those stories and we loved it. We were just such a close-knit family.

We've always been a bit of a clan. In times of trouble, we close ranks and we'd do anything for each other. Mum and Dad always steered it all. Their relationship has evolved, like any would do after so long together; Mum is now blind, and Dad is her absolute rock. But seeing their love and unconditional support for each other laid the foundations for me. It showed me just how solid real love could be.

When you're growing up, you don't really appreciate what your parents did until you're older and see what the world is really like. They did so much. Mum was only brought up with Grandma. There were no siblings, no aunts or uncles, no cousins. Living in the vicarage, she had all the protection of the Fathers. It was almost like a monastery there and yet she had the bravery to leave at such a young age and forge her own path. Her courage is something that would inspire me when I needed it most, later in my life.

For all the strong women in my family, much of those early years were dominated by men. There was a main vicar, Father Brown, who was in situ for the entire time Mum and Grandma were there. He was the patriarch really. I remember him as being stern and powerful. You wouldn't cross him. He was scary but you could see the love he had for my mum and my grandma and was always there for them, even when he became the Dean.

There were other fathers who lived there, some deacons, other priests to help, and those who were in training. It was a big church with thirteen bedrooms that could hold a lot of different people at one time. It was always busy. Grandma had her own quarters and to supplement her income, she would take on students to get some cash into the coffers. Often the money given by the parochial council didn't even cover the food and my grandma had very little money as a housekeeper.

The priests had their own dining room where they were served by Grandma, with Father Brown as the head of them all. When I was little, we used to sneak out of Grandma's quarters and go to the lounge and sitting room to press the old serving bells, which made Grandma run from room to room to see which of the Fathers wanted her! She was always at their beck and call, and she got very little recompense for it.

And where was Grandfather in all of this? Well, that's another story. We knew that he was Dutch, but we also knew that Grandma never wanted to talk about him. We just assumed he was dead.

There were no photographs or any memories of him at all. I remember in school having to produce a family history project and I wanted to do mine about her.

'I don't want some nosy teacher rooting about in my life,' she told me. It was very out of character as she was a loving and caring woman who was usually happy to chat about things, but she wasn't one for living her life in the public eye. I just parked the idea and accepted her stance. It was only about fourteen years ago that my mother was contacted by a lady who then told her she was her half-sister. Mum's father had been over here during WW2 and had gone back once it finished, to his family in the Netherlands.

The mother of the half-sister who contacted her was a nurse in Merthyr and he'd got together with Grandma shortly after, as well as having a family in the Netherlands. He and Grandma lived together as husband and wife. They couldn't have legally married but she did take his last name. When he went back after the war, the Dutch family had received letters from the Red Cross which had been written by Grandma when she had tried to contact him. I can understand now why she was reticent about opening that can of worms. She had the surname Le-Loux, she had a wedding ring, and after the war, Grandma needed money to support Mum and that's when she went to work at the vicarage. Mum remembers nothing before the vicarage, but she did have that paternal influence in her early years. It's still a story with so many chapters untold.

Everyone has a story to tell.

Mum's half-sister lives nearby and she went to the Netherlands to meet the family, coming back saying that my half-cousin is the absolute spit of me. It's bizarre to think you have that family out there that you know virtually nothing about. Grandma died suddenly after a heart attack. When she was in hospital on oxygen, she was trying to tell Mum some things but wasn't in any position to do that. In those days, there weren't so many single mums about and I do think Grandma was ashamed of it all, given the way she reacted about my family history project at school. There was no need for her to feel that way because I just had utter admiration for her. She had always put my mum first, while she was getting on with it and had probably lost the love of her life by whatever means. She was an incredible woman.

The mother of Grandpa's first illegitimate child got shipped off to Scotland so that no one would realise the age of the baby. As her own mother had been widowed a year before, there couldn't be the pretence that there often was in families as to who was the real mother. Mum's half-sister only found this all out when her own mum died and thinks there are probably more children out there.

All of these stories and many others that perhaps remain untold. But they all have a common theme: love.

The world was being ravaged by war. The futures of the characters had gone from one of certainty and predictability to one of worry and pain. Instead, they just grabbed happiness where and when they could before it was taken away from them. It would have been the same with so many others, who put aside the usual 'morals' of the time. Who'd blame them?

It was an interesting clash of the religious and the passionate, and I am blessed to have those incredibly strong women in my blood. Growing up, my parents were very traditional and this would have an impact on my formative years, and my years since.

There would have been no way that my sister Bridget or I could ever have lived with a man before marriage and having a child out of wedlock would have been incredibly frowned upon. None of those views ever came directly from my grandmother but the sense of it was certainly there. I sometimes wonder whether that is why I rushed into marrying my first husband.

We bought a house together before the wedding and I remember saying to my mum that we were going to stay over there. It was only about two weeks before the wedding, but she was totally against it. The irony was, a week later, Bridget came home and when we went for her final bridesmaid dress fitting, I was told she'd put on a bit of weight. I'd noticed she'd been throwing up a lot too and I went berserk in the dress shop as I was so worried about her being bulimic or anorexic. I never thought to put two and two together at that point, until a few days later when she said, 'I think I better do a pregnancy test.'

Two days before the wedding, we found out she was having a baby. She was 30 at that time. She had her own place in London, she was financially secure, yet her first thought was, 'Mum and Dad! How will I tell them?'

We both looked at each other. We'd both had Saturday jobs in chemists when we were younger and knew that you never get a false positive pregnancy test, ever, so I couldn't even say it might be wrong. 'Look,' she said, 'we're just going to have to bite the bullet. I'll do it before I go back to London.' She was most nervous about telling Dad, but truth be told, he was absolutely wonderful. Like I said, in times of trouble, we do close ranks and we'd do anything for each other.

He held her hand and told her, 'It's fine. We're here. We'll support you and we love you.'

Mum struggled. She rang Father Irving, our priest at St Martins at the time. 'For goodness' sake, Mary!' he chastised her. 'Why are you worried about what other people will think? She's your daughter and she's having a child – congratulations!' Mum still thought that this was the 1940s and that she had to be ashamed. My sister moved back, she had Mollie, and we all saw her baby as the little girl who brought Bridget home to us.

I had a lovely childhood. My parents were strong together and they worked really hard. Dad worked his way up and that was difficult. He was away a great deal, and I was brought up with that old cliché of 'Wait till your father gets home!' ringing in my ears for any minor transgression. When I was three, we moved to Newbury for Dad's job for about three years. Us kids then moved back to

Cardiff from Newbury and I stayed with Grandma while Mum was in Newbury with Dad. It made my bond with Grandma even stronger. I'd sleep in her double bed and rub her feet. In fact, I did that until I was about seventeen when I used to go round and see her with my friend before we went out clubbing! In my mind, I stayed with her for years, but my siblings tell me it was only a couple of months. It must have made quite the impression on me though.

We all returned to Cardiff and to the St Martin's family which felt like 'home.' Mum stayed with Dad a couple of days a week, but it really did feel like we were all where we needed to be. When I look back, I feel as if I had three incredibly strong maternal figures in my childhood – Mum, my sister, and my grandma. I carried forward many messages about women and their strength from what I saw and experienced in our matriarchal family.

Everything was a lesson and I was blessed to have been shown all of that strength and to know that we can bear enormous burdens and challenges in life. I'm not sure I've ever thought about that before. It all felt natural and normal; it's only on reflection it all becomes apparent. They gave me strong foundations to make me the woman I am today. Reflection brings that into sharp focus. It wasn't didactic; I just absorbed it. And it would help me when I too would face significant challenges of my own.

There was a degree of 'Catholic' guilt etched into our lives, even though we're not Catholic. If you don't go to Mass, or you can't do something, or you're not following the right things, there is a feeling of being less than you could (or should) be. It's a self-imposed guilt that I try very hard to get over. But as time has proven, it's almost impossible to shake off.

I became Head Chorister in the Church. I'd be out clubbing on a Saturday night then singing as a holy choirgirl at 10am on the Sunday after sleeping for just a few hours. That was normal life to me. It wasn't hypocritical, it was just normal teenage life with my faith thrown in for good measure. St Martins was so 'High Church' that visitors do tend to think it's Catholic. It's been called one of those 'bells and smells' churches - you come out and reek of incense. It's not one of those with guitars and drums and trendiness, it's an organ and someone swinging incense holders, censers, up and down the aisles.

However it was described, it would also be something that would play a huge part in my life while I went through challenges no one could ever imagine.

Chapter Two

Mr Schmooze

During my teenage years, the Church was just always there. It was part of my life. When I left for University in Swansea, I probably didn't have the same passion. There was a local church there which had a choir. Unfortunately, the rehearsals were on a Friday night and that didn't quite fit in with student partying! Until then, at home, I'd been able to do everything involving church, but I had to choose once I went to Swansea.

I always had my faith though. Even if I wasn't going to church, it was part of me. Going to St Martins wasn't like attending a religious ritual, it was just part of going home. Church was family. Historically, when Grandma had been working in the vicarage, she'd have to get the Sunday dinner ready for the priests, so she never went to earlier Mass at 10 am with all the singing as she was busy. If I was doing a solo at one of those, she would walk to the foyer of the church to listen to me, without going in and she'd then go back to her duties.

Sundays were huge for us as a family, and when Grandma retired, she would go to Mass at 8 am. Mum and Dad would then go to the 10 am service, and afterwards, we'd head to Grandma's for coffee and then bring her to ours for Sunday lunch. We'd discuss every topic under the sun before I'd return her home when I went back to evening Mass at 6 pm. We really did put the world to rights on those Sundays.

When Grandma passed away quite suddenly when I was 20, I struggled with my faith. I just wasn't sure for a while, and I questioned whether there was anything at all. Grandma had had a heart attack and died a week after Easter but, the week before that, had still been going to 8 pm Mass. The Good Friday before she passed away, she was in church with me.

When she died, I didn't feel God was being bad or evil in taking her away from me. There wasn't anger, just a questioning of was there anything after life? I felt I was letting my mum down by questioning these things. She'd just lost her mother, and I felt guilty about even thinking it. I certainly couldn't talk to anyone else in the family about questioning my faith at a time when we'd all just lost the matriarch of our family. Everyone was broken-hearted; they didn't need this on top of it.

A couple of weeks later, I went to Evening Mass, still questioning everything internally. There was a particular wooden statue in the corner of our church. It was in honour of St Martin giving half of his Roman centurion cloak to a beggar who eventually becomes

Jesus, becoming a saint as a result. After meeting Jesus, Martin gave up being a centurion and travelled to spread the word. Grandma had overseen the rota for the flowers that lay in front of the statue. I looked over my shoulder from the chapel I was in, and I saw somebody standing at the back of the church. I just turned round, not thinking anything of it. I mentioned to the server, 'Somebody came in halfway through the service. Were they OK?' I asked him.

He looked at me. 'Nobody came in.'

Somebody else independently mentioned it to the priest, who didn't know of my conversation with the server, and between us it felt like it was Grandma. It was as if she was there to tell me that I didn't have to question anything and that my faith was right. I felt settled from that point on.

When Grandma died, I was in my third year of university. I started off studying Business Studies, then changed to Law and came back to Cardiff after two years in Swansea. I was dealing with medicine and ethics when Grandma passed; in fact, I was studying all of the technicalities that I would later have to deal with in life, such as organ donation and who should have life-saving treatment.

After a law degree, you choose to go to the Bar or become a solicitor. I chose the latter. The main reason was that I didn't want to be self-employed after seeing how hard my dad had worked running his own company. That didn't work out as I'd expected as I was offered a partnership within two years of qualifying. If I had my time again, I would have become a barrister.

I was at school with a lad called Chris and everyone found it utterly amazing when we got together when I was 19. We were polar opposites; he was so quiet and quite happy with his lot whereas I had been Head Girl, I was in drama productions, I was sociable, and I was the life and soul of the party. I qualified as a solicitor and got married to Chris in the same month when I was 26. I thought we were in love, I really did, but we were just best friends who had helped each other through university and the loss of my grandma. Our families knew each other and there was just, overall, a settled nature to who we were together, although that was something that wasn't going to work for me.

We split up once when I was in law school and I think I confused the upset I felt as the loss of love, when it was actually the loss of a friend. There wasn't a bad bone in his body. We should never have got married but it was something that seemed like a natural progression. When you don't want to split up, you feel that you need to take a stand almost, and for us, that was marriage. I would never have moved in with Chris given my parents' views at that point. However, if I hadn't had my religious background, and if we had lived together, I don't think we would ever have got married.

I was career-driven. I'd just been made a partner. I needed to put my mark on the world whereas Chris was happy just moseying on through life. We were together for seven years in total but married less than two years before it ended. I think we just grew up. I did love him but was never in love with him. We split up around

Christmas 2004, then tried to pull it back for a couple of months before realising there was no point.

Bridget's birthday was in May and we decided to go away to Dublin for a trip. It was lovely; because I'd always been with Chris, we'd missed out on a lot of sisterly stuff. We planned to make up for it that weekend, starting with going out and having a great time. It was a wild first night, mostly at Temple Bar of course, and on the second night we went to a place recommended by someone I worked with, called the Bruxelles Bar in Harry Street. Bridget and I went outside to drink on the pavement and started having a good laugh together. All of a sudden, there were three guys next to us who began chatting to us.

There was a bloke called Stu, his best friend Steve who lived just outside Dublin, and Ewan, who was Steve's brother-in-law. Stu was just visiting Steve for the weekend. We started to talk to them, which veered off into me talking to Steve with Stu chatting to Bridget. Stu kept looking over at me and trying to get involved in my conversation with his friend, and it became very apparent that he was interested in me, not my sister!

I don't know how it came up, but I was telling Steve that I had a grand piano, when Stu interrupted with, 'I always knew my next girlfriend would have a grand piano.' Bridget rolled her eyes and said, 'Listen to Mr Schmooze here!'

He was unabashed. 'Where would you like to go for our honeymoon? How do you fancy the Maldives?' he asked me, still in the romantic environment of the pavement outside the pub! I was bemused by it all; even having someone chatting me up was unusual as I'd been with Chris for so long. I'd never been in this grown-up dating world.

Ewan butted in to ask if we'd like to go to some sort of rave club with them, somewhere outside of Dublin. It wasn't our scene at all, but we didn't say either way. As we walked away from the bar, there was a busker nearby. Stu was trying to impress me the whole walk, to little effect, and when he got his eye on the busker, he must have thought that was his opportunity to shine!

'Do you know any Crowded House?' he asked the bloke, who nodded, probably used to requests but no doubt wary of a gang of drunk people stopping in the street. 'How about Fall At Your Feet?' The busker nodded again, and before I knew it, Stu was serenading me! Bridget and I looked at each other. I had no idea where else to look, to be honest; this wasn't what I was used to at all.

'Come on,' she said, 'let's lose these guys. We'll get a cab and go back to Temple Bar.'

When Stu, Steve and Ewan saw us heading for the taxi rank, they tagged along with us, assuming that we were taking them up on their offer of the rave club. Bridget was rolling her eyes, so we got into a cab hoping to get away, but Steve jumped in beside us.

'Where you off to?' he asked.

Bridget grudgingly admitted we were heading for Temple Bar, and he shouted to Stu and Ewan for them to get another cab and meet us there. We were never going to shake them off at this rate! He was the ultimate wingman.

Stu managed to get me outside the bar and we had our first snog. I won't forget that. Then, later on, they got the 'vomit comet' back to Skerries. We'd all been knocking back pints of Diamond White and were well gone by then. Before we all split up, Stu asked for my number and I did actually give him my real one! He was the first bloke I'd ever done that with. Apparently, he tried to ring me that night but by the time Bridget and I got back to our room, the Diamond White had really kicked in and I couldn't have answered if my life depended on it. We got our flight early the next day, with Bridget calling Stu 'Mr Schmooze' the whole way back from Dublin. All I could remember was that I did fancy him, and that he was big. That was it.

It was back to Sunday lunch with our parents, during which there was a phone call.

It was Stu.

'I was just going to try you one last time,' he told me. 'I thought you'd been ignoring me.'

Bridget was mouthing, 'Is it Mr Schmooze?' as I spoke to him.

Stu was still in Dublin and started messaging me constantly from that point on. He lived in Birmingham and when he got back the next day, he asked if he could take me on a date. 'As if!' I told him. 'You're in Birmingham and I'm in Cardiff!'

'There are cars,' he told me. 'And roads . . . so, that'll work!'

He was true to his word and drove to see me, while I couldn't even remember what he looked like. He came to my house, actually. He stayed over; how trusting was I? But in between him asking me on a proper date and him coming to Cardiff, we were messaging a lot. The messages turned into phone calls, and the phone calls ended up being four or five hours a night. We just had that connection from the start. By the time he came down to Cardiff, I felt like I knew him. It also turned out that his ex-girlfriend was from Cardiff so he knew the place well. He booked a really nice Chinese restaurant down the Bay; he knew exactly what he was doing as he'd been there on many occasions! When he came down, there was something between us already. You couldn't help but trust Stu, he was just so open.

He turned up in a green Mini, the old-fashioned Mr Bean style, and he had a baseball cap on. When he got out, I wondered how he'd folded himself in! He had two bottles of champagne; we sat in the garden, and I was completely at ease. Everyone loved him. When we got a cab to go for dinner, he was immediately having full-on banter with the taxi driver. I went to the loo, and he was chatting with people at the next table and when I got back, he introduced me like we were an old couple! It didn't feel like a first date; we fitted from the start, but that doesn't mean I didn't have my walls up. I hadn't even finalised my divorce. I was worried about letting Stu in and falling in love. If my best friend could let me down, why wouldn't Stu?

As it turned out, he came to Cardiff to take me out and I never got rid of him. He drove back to Birmingham and we had another five-hour conversation that night. If I'd got that taxi with Bridget to Temple Bar on our own, my life would have been so different. If I hadn't picked up the phone on his one last try, everything would have changed.

Things got serious quickly but we were lucky. I was earning good money, which meant we could both afford to go on nice trips. My parents didn't even have to know he was there. It didn't look as if I was jumping into anyone else. We could have our relationship for us rather than worrying what others would say about it.

I later found out that Steve wasn't happy with any of this. He'd invited Stu to Dublin in the hope that his best friend would settle with one of his own girlfriend's six sisters and then move there. Instead, he met me! Steve was livid and I never heard the end of that.

Stu definitely knew that we were right for each other, but I also think he was incredibly lonely when we met. He blended into my extended world seamlessly. He enjoyed the fact that there was so much around my family. He had so much energy and was such a bundle of laughs and fun. I think people eventually thought that I was the way I was because of him, but in truth, he fell in love with me because it fitted with who he really was. I didn't rein him in, we were vivacious together and we grew together. He loved my singing and my amateur dramatics, he was the one who remembered every date of important times we spent together; he integrated himself into my world and by November 2006, he proposed.

It transpired that Stu had asked Dad for my hand in marriage. For the first time, we were having a family Christmas abroad. Mum, Dad, Bridget and her little girl, Mollie, Stu, and I were going to a chalet in Les Arcs to ski and, apparently, he was going to propose to me on the slopes at Christmas. That was what he had in his head anyway. Mum and Dad were celebrating their Ruby Wedding Anniversary on the 6th of November, and they planned to renew their wedding vows in church before we went. It was almost like another wedding reception in a local church hall. They'd invited 100 people including Stu's parents, who they'd already met. They'd said to him, 'If you propose when we're all away in France, there's no one there for you; there's no one from your side. It's about you starting off together and you need your family too. Wouldn't it be nice for you to propose when your parents are here as well?' It was their suggestion, but he was all for it.

He was so nervous that day and I had no idea why. I was trying to put up pictures of Mum and Dad while he was faffing about and just getting in the way. After the speeches, Stu said to me, 'Come outside for a minute, will you?'

He gave me a package. It was a copy of a book, but he'd wrapped over it and it said *The Story of Spanna and Stu* on the spine and cover. It started with a picture of where we met (we'd gone back to Dublin for the christening of Steve's little one the year before and he'd taken the picture then), of the car I drove back at the start, where I came from, the safari in Kenya, concert tickets, and so much memorabilia from all of our time together up until that point. It was full of all our little memories. It even had his first email to me. He knew – he'd known all along.

Then, a third of the way through the book, he'd carved out a square in the middle of the pages – and there sat an engagement ring. Stu went down on one knee when I got to that part and asked me to marry him. The ring was absolutely perfect. The most beautiful diamond I'd ever seen.

I had been so distracted with Mum and Dad's celebration that I hadn't seen it coming, which made it so perfect. It was genuinely out of the blue. We went back in and Dad made an announcement. They were incredibly proud and it was a gorgeous moment. I looked at the book then and saw it was a copy of Stephen King's *Desperation* and Stu had chosen it purely because it was thick enough to make the part for the ring. I had a real giggle at that - it was hardly a romantic choice.

A few weeks later, Stu was made redundant and he moved to Cardiff. I'd married Chris during summer months and very much wanted this to be totally different which was why I decided on a winter wedding for the next year. I was utterly in love and had ideas of a fairy-tale wedding which involved me designing my own dress. I wanted to be The Snow Queen from Narnia, with white fur around my collar and a stunning gown with Swarovski crystals underneath. We planned our wedding reception for Cardiff Castle in 2006. Father Irving was already our chosen priest but even though St Martins was so close to me, I'd married Chris there. I wanted to say my vows somewhere else. I didn't want to feel like it was being repeated. This was new, this was different. This was the real thing. We opted to get married in another local church and then to Cardiff Castle for the reception, with all of the same people going to both the ceremony and the party.

As I walked down the aisle, all I felt was excitement. When I got there, Stu said to me in a whisper, 'You won't believe it – the hotel has crashed my car and they've upgraded us to the Presidential Suite for free!' They had shown us around when we booked it, and it was about half the entire size of the upstairs floor overlooking Cardiff Castle.

'That was the bed Gene Pitney died in!' I whispered back. 'That's our honeymoon bed!'

When we went back to the suite, we invited loads of people back. By 3 am, Stu twigged it was our wedding night and threw everyone out – and I got over my morbid Gene Pitney thoughts!

We went to the Maldives for our honeymoon and, when we came back, Mum and Dad threw a huge party for everyone from church and I got to wear my dress again.

Life was perfect and I had no reason to expect it ever to be anything else.

Chapter Three

Fraser

Stu was such a romantic.

He was very loving. He would sign off every email with ILYWAMHMW – I love you with all my heart Mrs Wonderful, and I had that engraved in my wedding ring to him. When we got married, he always called me Mrs Wonderful. Every single morning, he would wake up and say, 'Good morning, Mrs Bates. I love you with all my heart. Every day I wake up with you is more special than the last.' That was every single morning of our time together. The grand gestures usually tinker off once you're married, but they never did with Stu, and he made me feel very much loved. He used to call us Linda and Paul; we were the McCartneys fighting against everyone else!

'I never want to spend a night away from you,' he would tell me, and true to his word, if he was working away, he'd happily drive back for four hours extra each way just to make sure he was home with me. We hardly spent any nights apart. He wasn't the kind of bloke who went to the pubs with his friends. We just did things together as a couple. I dragged him to the football a lot. He became part of my life here, and he never needed or wanted to do anything on his own.

It was a love story, it really was.

I had gone to see 'Love Actually' the night my first husband said he didn't love me anymore and that he was leaving. When I went back, I said to him, 'I want that movie love. I want all of that.'

'That doesn't exist!' he replied. 'You're seeking something that isn't there.'

'Maybe. But I still want it.'

When I met Stu, it wasn't immediate fireworks for me at all, but it was that movie love very soon. Back when I was finalising everything with Chris, he returned to what I'd said.

'What does Stu give you that I didn't?' he asked. It wasn't a horrible conversation; he was just trying to learn.

I knew the answer in an instant. 'He makes me feel beautiful.'

'I don't understand,' Chris said.

'That says it all – the fact that someone can make you feel beautiful on the outside and inside. He makes me feel a beautiful person in every way.'

Stu completed me. We just had such an amazing relationship and marriage.

He used to sing. He had his guitar with him at every party, he bought me drums for my 30th birthday, we had music in our life every day. It was just incredible and I felt so lucky to be his Mrs Wonderful. Of course, we fought but never over anything that really mattered, just petty things. I'd storm off to the park after an argument, thinking I'd been away for hours, and he'd have learned his lesson. But he wouldn't even have noticed I'd gone! We had five bedrooms in our house and I'd try to sneak off to one and stay annoyed at Stu, but he would follow me from bedroom to bedroom to make sure everything was OK before we went to sleep. We always made up before then.

We knew we wanted a family together from the start. Our relationship was intense quite quickly and, like children in a playground, we had names picked for about four or five future kids. By the time we married, we were in our thirties and I was the last one in the group of women I knew who hadn't yet had a baby. It didn't feel like pressure to get pregnant though, it was just a natural progression. Chris had thought a sticking plaster child might have fixed things for us, but I knew that I'd only have a child when it was right and that it was done out of, and into, love.

I don't even think Stu and I actually discussed it – we just knew we both wanted kids. By the time we got married, I was an equity partner in a law firm which made it the right time for me to think about it. I felt settled professionally and taking the next step to make a family fitted in really well. We began trying pretty much as soon as we were married but it seemed to take quite a while. Looking back though, I'm just impatient and don't have much concept of time! By the Christmas, it was my works do in the Cardiff Hilton, which was where we'd spent our wedding night. Mum did the wages for the company so she was there too. She kept saying, 'Spanny! Spanny! Have more turkey. It's good for you, it'll make you conceive!' She was in the background saying that all night.

I ate as much turkey as I could but was much more interested in the fact that 'Time of My Life' from Dirty Dancing came on.

'Right Stu,' I called to him. 'This one's for us – hope you've got your muscles ready!' We had to do the lift! I ran towards him 'baby-style' and backwards we went, with me whacking my head on the floor. I'm sure everyone else found it hilarious!

About a week later, I just felt like I was pregnant. I did a test on New Year's Day which was negative, but in my heart, I felt it was wrong. A few days later, it was positive as I'd expected.

'Was it that lift that got me pregnant?' I laughed at Stu. 'Did it take a whack on the head?'

'I'm not sure,' he replied, 'but this baby definitely needs 'Hilton' as its middle name!'

The pregnancy was a difficult one for a while as I bled a lot. We were back and forth to the hospital a great deal and I was sure, each time, that I'd lost the baby. I hadn't told anyone I was pregnant at that point, but I had to tell my business partner eventually as I was at the hospital so much and missing out on court a lot. Things did settle down and I became quite big pretty quickly. My sister-in-law was also expecting - her third baby - at the same time as me which was lovely.

We were sure it was a girl and the name we had was Libby Dot – not Hilton! I'd always wanted the name Martha but Martha Bates wasn't something I would do to my child! In Cardiff, everyone abbreviates names and with that surname Bates, we had to be careful as it had such connotations.

It was at the time we were discussing names that Cardiff City got through to the quarter-finals of the FA Cup. I turned to Stu and said, 'Come on then – we'll name our baby after the winning FA Cup goal scorer from City!'

'Yeah, right,' he scoffed. 'As if Cardiff City will ever get there!'

By the time of the semi-final, Stu was really nervous as they'd got through to that stage. 'Could we maybe make it the middle name, Spanna?'

'Maybe. Let's see!'

Pregnant and on the bus to Wembley for the Cup Final in 2008, I kept joking with him about our agreement, and, in turn, he kept reminding me he hadn't agreed to anything. I was a bit nervous myself! We'd gone through the squad list beforehand. I was secretly hoping for Aaron Ramsey. He was my favourite player and that was quite a nice name. Joe Ledley would have been fine too, especially as his girlfriend was our receptionist. Aaron Joseph would have been nice. I wasn't too enamoured with the names

Kevin McNaughton or Roger Johnson, who kept scoring. At that point, Stu was definitely not going to have Roger.

'It's a girl anyway,' he kept telling me.

I wasn't that passionate a fan that I would have named my baby after every squad member if we won the cup, but it was great to string him along.

In any event, we lost, and I definitely wasn't going to name my child after the Portsmouth player who scored. All of a sudden though, a boy's name popped into my head.

'If it's a boy . . .' I began.

'Which it won't be,' said Stu.

'Yes, but IF . . . why don't we go for Fraser, your middle name, and go for Aaron as the middle name?' It meant something from Stu's heritage and any little boy we had would have the initials FAB, which had to be a good sign!

'It's a girl though,' Stu insisted, rubbing my tummy. 'Aren't you, little Libby Dot?'

I remember tracking the baby's daily growth on a website – the stages from something not even visible on the head of a pin, to a watermelon that would need to get squeezed out somehow! When you really want something, and you see everyone around you getting it, there is a part of you that thinks what if I get a child and it's not what I imagined it to be. How will I feel?

With all of the spotting, I was transfixed by the weeks. I just needed to get this baby to a safe time. When would he be viable?

One of my best friends had her baby at twenty weeks. When I passed that, I thought I could breathe a bit more. I didn't wrap myself up in cotton wool, but mentally, I needed to get to that stage.

Everything we had for the baby was white as we didn't know the sex; there wasn't anything that was pink or blue. I also didn't want to tempt fate. The law practice had a flat right opposite in which we stored archives. When Stu's parents bought us our pram, an old-fashioned-style Silver Cross, I kept it there in line with all the old wives' tales that it would be bad luck to have it in our home. We only bought enough clothes for the first few days; nothing was taken for granted after all the bleeding we'd endured.

I stopped work on the 1st of September. For the first week, I was going insane with boredom. Going from being a partner in a law firm to just sitting and waiting for a baby to arrive was another world. One of the things we did to pass the time was to have a competition to see who could get more friends on Facebook. We posted all the time just as part of that little competition between us – videos, memories, day-to-day life, and I am so grateful for it all now, so grateful. We must have looked remarkably annoying as if we were posing for everything and posting to show off, but it was really just us. I look back now, and I am thankful for every single post as they all mean something.

I suddenly went into labour watching 'The Fugitive' on the 14th of September 2008. 'I'm having the baby!' I shouted, jumping up. 'I'm having the baby.'

I went for a bath while Stu rang the hospital, and within a couple of hours, we were there and they didn't even measure me.

'Why aren't you checking how dilated I am?' I asked after about half an hour.

'There's no point. You're in labour and well on your way!' I was told. I'd had dreams of a serene water birth and they did get the pool ready. I went in and everything seemed fine but when it was time to start pushing, there was meconium everywhere. Straight away, I was whisked off to theatre where they decided a forceps delivery was needed. I'd only had gas and air and needed an epidural very quickly before theatre. All of a sudden, I was in there with my legs in the air and a bit shell-shocked.

'Whose legs are those?' I asked the surgeon.

'Yours!'

I couldn't stop giggling. It was surreal. With the last forceps attempt, they managed to get my baby out.

'It's a boy!' a midwife said before whisking him off to suck the meconium out of his lungs. It felt like forever until he started to cry and they weren't telling me anything at all. It was the first time ever I had seen Stu quiet.

After he began crying, they handed my baby to me for skin-to-skin contact and to feed him straightaway.

Not Libby Dot, but Fraser Aaron.

My boy.

Born on the 15th September.

Stu was peering on, a little bit ashen about what must have been a scary thing for him to witness as we got moved to the recovery ward. I had a fourth-degree tear and had lost a lot of blood. The forceps had not treated me kindly but all I felt was relief that my baby was safely here. I felt blessed after the trauma of what had happened so suddenly. Everything was OK; we were a family and we had survived that scare. It would be the three of us against the world and it felt completely right.

When I was in the recovery room, all I could think about was something that had happened ten days before my due date. I remember bumping into a lady from church who had been an assistant on a midwifery ward.

'Rhea, I'm really struggling at the moment,' I told her. 'I love my husband so much. How am I going to love my child as much as I love him?' I admitted.

She turned to me and said, 'When you have a child, another piece of your heart grows – a piece you never even thought was there.'

She was right. It had happened. My heart had grown instantly. I didn't have to decide who to love, or treat them differently. My heart had actually got bigger. It was so ready to accommodate this beautiful child that was part of us, a part of Stu, a part of me.

Fraser completed us. There was such a beautiful, immediate bond between me and Fraser, between all three of us.

He was huge – not in weight, he was 8lbs, but the length of him was remarkable! He had a head of dark hair and blue eyes. He did have marks on his head from the forceps (although they disappeared quite quickly) and he was just beautiful.

I had to stay in hospital for a few days after the birth just to make sure I was ready to be sent home. Father Irving had asked if he could be there at the birth. That might sound odd, but he was always there at the end of life, he was always there for death, and he just wanted to experience the full cycle. Stu had said, 'With respect, I just want it to be us.' However, he was the first one to visit and I remember him even holding my vomit pot for me!

Fraser never really seemed like a baby. It was almost as if he had been here before, a little Benjamin Button. The first few weeks, yes, he was obviously a baby and breastfeeding was a nightmare, but he still had an air about him. He was hungry all the time and the health visitor told me to put him on formula, which settled him completely. We christened him in the December and, at that point, at less than four months, he was already rolling about.

For Christmas, we went to Stu's parents who lived in a converted old stately hall which had a lounge that was the old ballroom. I put Fraser on the floor to let him wriggle about and he rolled from one side of that massive room to the other. We went skiing in the February after he was born. He grew out of his baby sling so quickly and was in a rucksack on my back by the time we went to the slopes. At eight months, we went to Crete on holiday and had to dress him in proper clothes. If we'd put him in a babygro, people would have thought we were mad – he looked like a child, not a baby. He had spikey hair, he was very mobile, he was just sorted already! All the other children on that holiday spoke to him as if he was a toddler, simply because they assumed he was. He had so much character from the start. He was a bundle of fun, full of energy, from the beginning. We could see the child he was going to be.

Fraser had been here before. We were sure of it.

Chapter Four

Another Pregnancy

Being thrown into motherhood was life-changing. I had that initial love and bond, but there was a lot of learning to be done in those first few weeks. Everyone wants to tell you how to parent, but as an older parent, I was perhaps let off the hook a little in terms of not being patronised quite as much as many other mums are. It became obvious very quickly that Stu, Fraser and I, weren't going to be a bath-bottle-bed sort of family. It was finding a way between what people tell you that parents do, and what is right for you.

I don't think we had much of a routine, and Fraser never really settled to start with anyway. Families either do things their way or how society tells them, and I wanted a routine but it never worked for us. As Fraser rolled around so quickly and was hungry so quickly, I don't think we could have stuck to the parental calendar! He was even acting as if he was starving at his own christening when he was only about three or four months old, and I felt a naughty mum giving him a bit of food, but the poor child was desperate for it! He just wasn't satisfied and had his own ideas about what was right for him and at what time it should be happening.

Although I didn't want that bath-bottle-bed routine, I had to organise some things such as childcare. We found a lovely childminder and I just assumed everything would be sorted. I'd drop Fraser off every morning and trot off to work, pick up my career, and all would be well.

That first morning showed me just how wrong I'd been.

The emotion and pain I felt was something I'd never imagined. I cried all the way to the office. I never thought I'd be that maternal. All I could think was that I didn't have my baby with me. It didn't matter that the childminder was brilliant – I was away from my little boy. Stu had organised it so that he would do the pick-up at 4.30 pm every day and that gave him time with Fraser until I got back in the evening. We did dual parent, but I just wanted my baby and was shocked by the amount of love I had.

Stu was more nervous as a parent. I always say he had the nerves for both of us, but we just loved Fraser with all our hearts. I never even had a doll when I was growing up, I had no interest. Instead, I went to the football with my dad, I played football with my brother - that was much more interesting than a dolly and a pram. It wasn't that I was a tomboy or however you want to categorise it; I just enjoyed doing everything no matter what the gender expectations were. I wasn't what society might have thought a girl who wanted a baby would be. I didn't crave a little girl, but I was now faced with all of this love for my son. It knocked me sideways. Fraser just became part of our world, he did everything with us, and it was the best thing.

I couldn't believe that I had questioned whether I would feel love for him, that I had questioned whether I might feel a bit resentful that a baby would take some of Stu's focus off me. Stu had always put me on a pedestal. I'd thought I might lose that, as well as my role as Mum and Dad's little girl, their baby. I'd worried I just wouldn't connect. I also thought that I would want to be the best mum; what if I wasn't? I was worried about being a failure and here I was now, aching for him.

Stu and I used to argue about who first called him 'Bear.' It was definitely me though! We had a department store called House of Fraser here in Cardiff and they used to have their own brand of teddy bears, and I'd grown up with having toy cuddly Fraser bears. Stu and I also loved everything to do with Bear Grylls and Fraser Bear just became what we called him, then it was Bear for most of the time. On the back of his first football shirt were his initials FAB – but that could just as easily be Fraser Aaron Bear as much as it could Bates. He looked like a bear and he cuddled like a bear. It just seemed completely natural to call him that.

I walked Fraser everywhere, so much so that the wheels of the pram fell off. I was always with him. He was like a koala bear.

He was always loving, very charismatic, cwtchy, and everyone started to call him Bear, just like everyone calls me Spanna. That had started when I was a child, and Anna-Louise was a bit of a mouthful for my siblings. They added to it to make fun of me, and I became Anna Louise Spanna Cheese. First, the 'cheese' got dropped, then the 'Anna-Louise,' and I was just left with Spanna or Span or Spanny. If I was out clubbing and someone asked why I was called that, I'd say my dad was a mechanic, or he owned Spanair Airlines – it wasn't the nicest nickname in the world, but I just accepted it. My hen night T-shirts said, *Spanna's Hen Night* on the front, and *Lend us your tool!* on the back. One of the first things Stu ever said to me was, 'Is your sister calling you Spanna?'

'Yeah, she is,' I admitted.

'And don't you think that's a bit . . . offensive? It means dull, doesn't it?'

'It's just what everyone calls me.'

He ended up calling me it, and so did his family. In fact, even Father Irving calls me that. If my parents call me Anna-Louise, I know I've done something wrong. And, similarly, if I ever said, 'Fraser Aaron Bates!' he'd be in trouble, although he rarely was.

Fraser loved toy cars and you could sit him with a load of them and he'd play happily on his own for hours. He became quite a theatrical child very early on, doing his own shows from a really young age. When he was about two and a half, he started to sing a lot. Obviously, I'd always sung to him but when he got to that age, he was belting songs out. In the early days, when he wouldn't settle, I played piano and sang to him all the time, I think it might have soothed me more than him and, when he got older, I continued to do it every night before bed as he wasn't so keen on bedtime stories. One of our lullabies was 'Castle on a Cloud' from 'Les Miserables' – 'There is a castle on a cloud, I like to go there in my sleep . . . I know a place where no one's lost, I know a place where no one cries, crying at all is not allowed, not in my castle on a cloud.'

It's a really poignant song where Fantine dies and her daughter, Cosette, has to go and live with people who don't care for her. Instead of Cosette, I would change it to, 'She says, Fraser, I love you very much,' and he loved that. The other song we loved was 'Caterpillar in a Tree' from Hannah Montana, a song that is sung after she's lost her mother and her father is trying to guide her through who she can be. Now, again, I look back on those lyrics and they mean so much –

'Butterfly fly away, butterfly fly away.

Flap your wings now you can't stay, take those dreams and make them all come true.

Butterfly fly away, butterfly fly away.

We've been waiting for this day. All along and knowing just what to do,

Butterfly, butterfly, butterfly, butterfly fly away.'

Songs did settle Fraser. They did calm him down, as did the theme from Hollyoaks which I used to have on in the background while I was feeding! When he started singing, I could tell he was pitch perfect, he could hold any tune. Like Stu, he only needed to hear something once and he could remember it.

Once Fraser started school, I said to his teacher, 'He's not reading you know, he's just remembering it and reciting the book back to you.' That was how his mind worked. He was unbelievably good at singing and had the voice of an angel. I have recordings of him singing 'Fix You' with Stu and he was getting all of the beats right as well. This tiny little boy sitting on a seat next to his dad, duetting as if it was the most natural thing in the world.

Stu had learned to play the guitar by ear, whereas I was classically taught and I could see that Fraser had his dad's flair. Stu and I used to sing a lot together and I had been his duet partner when he did gigs or weddings or parties; basically, that meant me singing all the end bits on songs (the token woman from Deacon Blue, or the nah-nah-nah-nah bit on '500 Miles'). We sang constantly around the house and we had Sing Star on the PlayStation. It was constant in our house; we were a family full of love and music and laughter.

I had been the main breadwinner when I was a lawyer and when I left, it did shake our little family up. Stu had to also think about his career. He was in IT working as a project manager and, after a little while, I went to work at another practice where I didn't have the responsibility of being in charge of absolutely everything. It allowed me to make another decision.

'Maybe now would be a good time to think about having another child,' I said to Stu.

I got pregnant very quickly this time and, again, I knew before I got a positive pregnancy test result. We were back in Dublin to see Stu's best friend and I said to his wife, 'I'm sure I'm pregnant.' She made me promise to do a test and tell her, but it was negative. A few days later, that had changed, and our second baby was on the way! Thankfully, I didn't have any bleeding during that pregnancy.

I stopped working in the December and the baby was due in June. It was lovely to have that time with three-year-old Fraser, just the two of us. It was tough to leave the law completely and I even questioned whether Stu would still love me. After all, when we'd met, I was a partner in a law firm. I was dynamic, I was ambitious, but now I had lost my confidence; I was a bit adrift. I couldn't help but think I wasn't the woman he had fallen in love with. I had lost what I had worked hard for, and what I had achieved at such a young age. It was gone so quickly and that was tough. Had I defined myself by my job? I hoped not, but how did other people view me now? I did learn to be the new me, however, and of course, Stu still loved me.

'I've changed so much,' I said to him. 'I'm not who I used to be.'

'You haven't changed at all,' he replied, hugging me. 'I fell in love with you, not your job.' It was just what I needed to hear. I had so much joy in my heart and even though we didn't have much money, it was the happiest time of my life.

Chapter Five

Elizabeth and Fraser

We managed to get to the Football League Cup Final again when I was pregnant with our new baby – and we had the same deal! We'd name our secondborn after the winning goal scorer, and we'd definitely keep to it this time! We played Liverpool that time and Joe Mason was the first to score. I loved the name Joseph, so that was fine if things stayed that way – we'd go for Joseph Spencer Paul Bates. Ben Turner scored again in extra time, and there was then a penalty shoot-out in which Don Cowie and Peter Whittingham scored, but it didn't matter as Liverpool hit the back of the net more than us. We'd have to get our baby's name elsewhere!

Whereas with Fraser, Stu could often come to appointments, he was the main breadwinner now and there were many times I had to go alone. It was quite sad, but our circumstances were very different. Due to my age – I was 36 at this point – I had a lot more medical involvement. I didn't want to risk an amnio because of the risk of miscarriage and I already had a history of bleeding during pregnancy with Fraser, so we chose a nuchal fold test to see if the baby had Down's Syndrome as I was an older mum, but it came back as something like 1 in 100,000.

Again, we didn't choose to find out the sex, but at the scan there appeared to be a willy. When the next appointment came and they checked the heartbeat, I had in my mind the old saying, *If it's a train, it's a boy; if it's a galloping horse, it's a girl*, and it was definitely a train! My midwife said, 'Why are you so convinced it's a boy?' I showed her the scan and she laughed. 'OK, I get your point!' Joseph Spencer Paul (after my dad) Bates was on his way.

I had another worry this time though, again about love. Fraser was such a bundle of energy. He was so much fun and I adored him. How could another boy make me feel that way? It was never the worry about having three males in the household; it was just this worry about how could I not compare a new boy to Fraser? Fraser was sure I was wrong about bringing another boy into the mix anyway. He was the only one who was insistent he was having a sister. He would kiss my tummy and talk to 'her.' He was sure from the start, but we'd all seen the scans and heard the heartbeat.

About two weeks before the birth, I found out the baby was breech and I was referred to hospital. Mum came with me to the appointment and, because of the difficulties with Fraser, I felt I should have been consulted with on whether I wanted an elective caesarean. The tear, the repair, and the severity of it all had been horrendous but I just thought I'd have to do it again. Once I started to speak to the consultant and say to her that the baby was breech, she did an examination and told me, 'No – I'm not sure the baby is breech actually.'

'Could I maybe have a scan to check?'

Begrudgingly, I was given one that confirmed what the midwife had said. I went back to the consultant who said, 'I suppose it is, but I can book you in and get it turned.'

'I don't want that at all! The baby could turn back. Fraser got into so much trouble. With the benefit of hindsight, I think he was trying to turn and that didn't go well at all. My brother was breech too so maybe it runs in the family. I think I'd like a caesarean.'

As soon as I said that, she turned to my mum and said, 'Well, can you talk to her about having the baby naturally?'

Mum stared her down and told her, 'What I went through? I wouldn't wish that on my worst enemy, let alone my own daughter.' When Mum had Martin, she'd been rushed into hospital. They had tried to turn him and when he was born, without Dad being there as that wasn't allowed back in 1969, they suspected Martin had brain damage from the birth. Eventually, they decided he was fine, but she'd been through so much with it.

The consultant asked me, 'Do you actually understand what a caesarean involves?'

'Of course I do. I've read a lot.'

'From the internet I suppose?'

'No. I'm a lawyer and I need to know about medical procedures for that.'

'Why? What do you specialise in?'

'Personal injury and medical negligence.'

Never in the history of obstetrics has a caesarean been booked in so quickly I imagine! I'd never used the lawyer card before, but my goodness, I'm glad I did that day. The section was scheduled for June 25th - ten days before the due date, and ironically, the night before, I started having contractions. They came to nothing and we dropped Bear off at nursery the next morning. Off we went, with a CD loaded with a birth playlist for when I was under the knife. Just as he'd been with Fraser's birth, Stu was terrible!

'You can go down and see the baby coming out,' he was told.

'Oh no, no, no, no! I'm staying up this end!'

'Don't look up in the steel lights then. You don't want to see a reflection of her cut wide open!'

He was too scared that he didn't even remember to give the playlist in. I could see his petrified eyes above the mask! He managed to hold my hand and that was about it.

We'd told the midwife when we went in that we were having a little boy, and all they told us when the baby came out was, 'Here's your baby!'

'Is everything OK?' we asked.

'Yes! But look! Look!'

'What?'

'It's a girl!'

I screamed. I didn't realise until that moment how excited I was to be the mummy of a little girl, as it hadn't even entered my mind until then that it might be possible.

Elizabeth Dorothy.

She'd be Libby Dot just as we'd planned with our previous pregnancy but, again, Fraser had his own ideas. He walked in to see her and immediately said, 'Hello Elizabeth!' and she was never Libby at all. He had been the one who had known a little girl was coming and he was the one who decided what she was going to be called. To this day, she will proudly tell people that her big brother named her.

We had taken in some plain babygros in white and beige for the new arrival, but that wasn't enough for Stu! He left the hospital and bought everything he could in Boots that was pink. It was a world of it! By the time my sister came in later, she said, 'Could you get any more pink on that baby?'

I put Elizabeth straight on the bottle, and she pretty much slept straight through that first one. When we got home, she slotted in perfectly. I'd armed myself with a boxed set of Downton Abbey for the night feeds but never needed to even take the cellophane off, she was that good, settled and easy. She was as bald as a coot; there was no chance of getting little girly hairclips and bows on her head! She looked so cute with a hat on, but when that came off, her baldness was a bit of a shock. I was used to my hairy little Bear, but not with Elizabeth.

Fraser adored his new little sister. Our family of three became a family of four easily; she was the icing on the cake. They were 'mini-mes' apart from their eyes – Fraser looked like his Dad but had my eyes, Elizabeth looked like me but had Stu's eyes.

Not long after Elizabeth's birth, Stu got promoted and I became a Slimming World consultant. That gave me some confidence back as I felt I was helping people again. I was being me once more and I could see results. Stu really supported that. I could fit it around two kids, he could carry on with his career, and I loved the life we had at that point. I really enjoyed it and felt like I'd got a bit of my identity back. It did me such a lot of good to get my confidence back and have some time with other adults out with the children. I didn't want to go back into law at all. I did find that a few of my slimming group wanted a lot of free legal advice, but that was as far as it went!

Elizabeth was an easy baby but certainly saved it all up to be a difficult toddler! She soon joined in with the dancing in the kitchen, the music that we sang and played everywhere, races on the floor with them on our backs; it was the loveliest life. To outsiders, we probably looked like that annoying family who had it all – and we did. I never once thought it was all too perfect. I just thought we'd have it forever. I was blessed and I was an optimistic person anyway. Why would things change? I was appreciative though as there was a lot of sadness on the outskirts of our lives.

The February before Elizabeth was born, our close friend lost her one-year-old son and then her husband had taken his own life. Another woman in our neighbourhood got hit by a bus crossing the road in Swansea, leaving behind three children. To the right of us, we had a young girl who was on a boat in Thailand when it sank. Another neighbour lost her son in a freak accident. Stu's work colleague's son was run down by a drugged driver in Cardiff. We seemed to hear a lot about these freak incidents and this all happened in a really short space of time.

The estate we were living on was built on an old factory that had stored nuclear bombs. We used to joke and say our house was the one that glowed, but if everyone in the street had suddenly contracted cancer, you would have thought there was maybe a reason. But all of these incidents were something else. It was bizarre.

With me being at church, I grew up around death. The choir sang at more funerals than weddings. I was very aware of the fragility of life. I appreciated every single moment I had and the level of love that was around me. Stu always said that the most precious thing you could give was your time. His school motto had been **Fidem vita fiteri**, which is Latin for *Show your faith by the way you live*. Dad had raised me to believe in the saying, *Work hard, play hard*, and those were the sayings we lived by.

Fraser continued to be a very grounded sort of little boy who always knew his place in the world. He could be best friends with a baby or a pensioner, it didn't matter. He just had such a caring nature that I don't think I could ever sum up. He wanted everyone to be happy.

At primary school, there were twenty boys and eight girls in his class. He was the biggest, very sporty, very charismatic, and you would have thought he would have been competing for that alpha male role, but he didn't. He was a friend to everyone. He looked after a little boy with hearing difficulties, he protected a boy who was often bullied, but he himself never got anything bad hurled at him. He saw the good in everyone; he never said a bad word about anyone. He was just the kindest boy.

They had a fundraising non-uniform day in school for one of Fraser's friends, Oscar, who had a rare blood condition. The money was going to LATCH, the Welsh children's cancer charity who had really supported the family. Fraser made his own outfit and it was of a superhero lion, with 'O' for Oscar as Oscar was a superhero in Fraser's eyes for going through so much. That was Fraser's attitude to things; he always acknowledged people and cared for them.

When he saw the Paris atrocities on TV, he was so upset and wanted to check on a boy he knew who had been to Paris.

'Is he OK?'

'He's fine, Bear. He isn't there now. He was there on holiday.'

'Are you sure? What if he's there? What if people are hurting him too? Why are they doing that?' He really struggled with the idea of people being cruel.

His favourite football player was Duncan Edwards and that was because he was so drawn to the story of the Munich Air Disaster in which eight Manchester United players died in 1958. Duncan Edwards had initially survived but later died of his injuries.

On the odd occasion when Stu stayed away, Fraser would come into my bed. 'I'm the man of the house tonight, Mum,' he'd say. 'I'll look after you.' It felt like he was way older than his years. He had the biggest heart.

Singing and dancing filled every day. We all played football together and we loved to watch films as a family, all cwtched up on the sofa. He adored Star Wars. I'd put it on and, with Stu, they'd be transfixed, knowing every scene, every line. He'd watch Top Gun with me, one of my favourites, and I'd cough every time I knew there was a swear word coming.

One day, Fraser took my hand as we were watching and said, 'It's alright Mum, you don't have to cough. I do understand there are swear words and it's fine!'

However, his favourite film was called 'Believe' which involves Sir Matt Busby dealing with the aftermath of the Munich Air Disaster and coaching a local football team to try and help him to deal with the grief. Fraser was only five or six when he locked onto his interest in that topic, and after watching it once, it needed to be on a loop. He never had many questions about such a hard topic, he didn't even really go into detail; he was just so absorbed in the topic. When we went on a cruise when he was six, he had his Duncan Edwards T shirt on all the time, and he'd already had his interest in the topic for a while. People would say, 'Oh, you're a Manchester United fan! Who's your favourite player?'

When such a little boy replied, 'Duncan Edwards,' they were taken aback. These old men were bamboozled, expecting him to say Ronaldo! That was the film that led him to his favourite song, 'Forever Young' too. He'd make activity courses to complete, he'd dribble the football to the local shop when we went, he was always outside. He tried to make everyone happy. His paternal grandfather had played for Aston Villa, my dad for Cardiff Boys, a friend of ours loved Celtic, so he always tried to wear the shirt that would please that person.

Fraser adored any Italian food, spaghetti bolognese or pizza, but his favourite thing in the world was Maryland cookies. When we went on a cruise in 2015, we took ten packets with us to keep him going. We'd barely reached Venice when they were all done! He wouldn't even consider the ones they made on the ship, so spent a day traipsing around Venice to every little shop and supermarket. We finally found a local brand that didn't quite hit the mark with our Cookie Monster, but he had to suck it up. On that holiday, the cruise ship band who had been brought in, The Zoots, asked for someone to come up and play air guitar with them – the first time they'd ever requested that apparently. Fraser's hand was up like a shot, and when he got up on that stage, it looked like he was born for it. For the rest of the cruise, everyone recognised him and stopped him to say 'hello' to the famous Fraser!

My sister-in-law's grandmother was psychic and was quite well-known to a lot of celebrities. She met Fraser on a handful of occasions and always had such a special affinity with him. Each time they met, she'd say to my sister-in-law, who had her own children, 'He's very special that boy, a very special young man.' No one could quite put their finger on the bond they had. I thought it was lovely but thought no more about it.

One time, we were going to Birmingham to stay with Stu's old university friends and Fraser was only about three and didn't comprehend where we were off to or what the trip would involve (apart from a day at Thomas Land). On the morning before we set off, he came running into our bedroom and said, 'We can't go. Wherever it is, we can't go.'

'What do you mean?' I asked, cuddling him. 'Why don't you want to go?'

'No, we *can't* go – there's been an accident,' he told me.

'We're all fine, really we're fine.'

'But there's been an accident,' Fraser repeated.

We thought nothing of it, got ready and put him in the car. We started to drive towards the M5 and my mum rang.

'Are you OK?' she asked. 'I'm just checking because there's been a huge pile-up on the motorway just before Thomas Land.'

It made us both go a little bit cold. It sent a chill through us. Had he known? Was there something there he was aware of? I did wonder about this little boy who seemed to have been here before, and how any gift he might have would show itself as he grew.

I could only wait and see.

Chapter Six

The Party

Stu started to get really unsettled about his job. He had a feeling that he was going to be made redundant. I thought he was worrying about nothing. In fact, I felt he was going to be promoted, but it niggled at him a lot. I did try to support him going through those worries, but they seemed misplaced to me. Even if he was right, we'd find a way through it.

I took charge of my Slimming World meeting one night and when I came back, he was really agitated.

'I've just been watching The Pride of Britain Awards,' he said. 'Jess just got one. You really need to watch it.'

'I'm not being funny Stu, but no, I don't watch that sort of thing. I'll be in pieces.'

'You must, you must!'

'No, I mean it. Absolutely not.'

The Saturday after that, we had my parents around for Dad's birthday. Somehow, the topic came up again.

'Did you watch The Pride of Britain Awards?' Stu asked them. 'Our friend Jess was on it – she donated her son Teddy's kidney. I've signed up to make sure that, if anything happens to me, I want to be an organ donor.' He was really emphatic about it.

'Stu! Can we please not talk about this?' I asked. 'We're having a nice family meal, it's not right.'

'Why not? Why won't you talk about it?'

'It's just a bit – well, it's icky. Fraser's around, Elizabeth is running in and out, I just don't want to.'

'We must Spanna, we must talk about it.'

Dad then said, 'Stu, why have you signed up? There's no point. The opt-out scheme is coming in soon. You don't need to say you'll donate any more, you only have to say if you specifically don't want to.'

'I want this conversation,' he reiterated.

'Wait a minute,' I interrupted. 'What do you mean we have to opt-out? What does that mean?'

'Father Irving's not keen,' said Mum. 'He's not impressed at all. The Government telling us what to do again, not giving us the choices.'

'That's ridiculous,' replied Stu. 'You can opt out. And anyway, everyone should donate their organs.'

The conversation started to get quite heated. We'd had a glass of wine, and everyone was making their point. We moved onto something else eventually, but I now knew very, very clearly what Stu wanted if the worst ever happened.

On our anniversary, four days later, I organised a night away for both of us at a hotel in Cardiff. We hadn't done that since Elizabeth had been born. Our friend messaged us to say she'd been in our very suite the night before for the launch of the organ donor opt-out. We also bumped into the CEO of Stu's company, and I could see in the way that man interacted with him, that there was no way they were going to make Stu redundant. We were going to be fine.

'Shall we go on the Big Wheel?' I whispered to Stu as we held hands and walked around. That was a bit of a tradition for us. When we'd got married, the idea was that all of our guests would come with us to the Christmas Winter Wonderland before we went into Cardiff Castle for the reception. We gave them all candles for when we came out of the church and for the walk to the Big Wheel; it was such a beautiful moment, but it also turned out to be absolutely freezing. I was wrapped up in my Snow Queen cloak and dress; I was fine, so only Stu and I did it. It was the most amazing memory and we got some incredible photographs, and it became a bit of a tradition every time the Winter Wonderland came to town.

'Maybe we could get some time away together more often,' Stu reflected. It was the first time we'd left the kids overnight and it did feel like a bit of a watershed. They were getting older and it might be the moment where Stu and I could be on our own sometimes. 'We could do this,' he said, kissing the top of my head.

We had our whole lives ahead of us as a family, but as a couple too.

Christmas was coming and, for Stu, that was the best time of year. He always loved dressing up and he adored being Father Christmas, to the extent that he had his own costume. He had become the Father Christmas for Fraser's nursery then his school, then Elizabeth's nursery. On Saturday 5th December, he was going to be Father Christmas for Lisvane Primary just as he'd been the year before. This year, however, no one was going to be free, so I offered to be his elf. I got a costume and the night before, we all watched Elf. Stu was so exhausted that he fell asleep on the sofa and I cuddled up with the kids.

The following morning, Fraser had football as usual and we headed off to the school fair to prepare. One of the other parents would bring Fraser along later. He and Elizabeth had absolutely no idea that their dad was Father Christmas! They knew I was the elf, but they didn't question anything at all. We were keeping the magic alive for Fraser and I did wonder whether this might be the last year that he would believe before someone burst his bubble.

It was a great day and I met a lot of the parents I'd never met before. I used to do drop off and pick up, probably keeping myself to myself a bit, and certainly not knowing the parents in other years. But this was new for me; I met so many of them. Stu and

I had such a good laugh that day - it really was a lot of fun. We finished up about 4 pm and got ready for a charity Christmas jumper party that evening in a friend's house. We'd been before and Stu had always driven, but on this occasion, I thought he should have a break.

'Why don't we just drop the car off? You've been having a hard time, just let your hair down for one night and have a drink. We can collect it on Sunday and go to Father Christmas duties at Elizabeth's nursery tomorrow?' I said to him.

It was my idea.

It was all my idea.

We arranged to stay with our friend after the party and get up early the next day to do all of our other plans. The four of us drove to my friend's in Miskin and started to relax a bit. My friend's boyfriend told us, 'We'll drive the cars there, leave them, walk back here after the party then Stu can come with me in the morning to get them.'

We all had our Christmas jumpers on and Stu had his Father Christmas costume in the back of the car. He was in his element. He even had his Christmas pants on! For some reason, at my friend's house, Stu started showing some videos of me singing at my parent's Golden Wedding.

'I'm so proud of Span,' he told them. 'Just so proud of her.' I'd sang Panis Angelicus at the event which was the first time I'd performed properly since Ave Maria at my sister's wedding when

I was eight months pregnant with Fraser. God knows how I'd managed the breathing for that! It had been seven years between the two and Stu had recorded it all.

'If you two get married, Spanna can sing – listen to her!' I did feel that he was really proud of me and it was lovely.

We followed my friends to the party and I remember it took about ten minutes to drive there. 'You said it was really close,' I said when we got there.

'Oh, it's a lot quicker to walk back,' she replied. 'Don't panic about that, it's just driving that takes longer - you have to go a longer way round. It'll be much quicker when we walk back later tonight.' I'd taken Elizabeth's stroller in the hope that she'd fall asleep when we did head back to my friend's house to stay overnight. That way, we'd all be sorted for a lovely night and a planned walk home in preparation for Christmas.

Finally, we all arrived at the house for the traditional party where Stu was going to be Father Christmas yet again. It was a real family event and the year before, there must have been about fifty kids who'd had their photos taken with Stu. Once you'd had a Stuey Father Christmas experience, you wanted one every year after that!

As soon as we got there, Fraser and Elizabeth went upstairs to play with the other kids, but my little boy was soon back down again. He was very clingy that night and didn't really want to leave my side. He was extremely caring too; he wanted to be with me rather than the other children or enjoy the party atmosphere. It was as if he just needed to be with me, as if he knew that something was coming. My friend's daughter Amelia was older and very good with kids and she took charge of Elizabeth, leaving me to be with Fraser for most of the evening.

Stu came up and said, 'It's time.'

I prised Fraser from me, wondering how I'd explain this. I wanted to keep the magic for a little longer so told him, 'Father Christmas is really busy getting gifts sorted tonight and he's asked Dad if he can help out. Don't tell the other children though – it's just something for us to know. Our secret!' You could see that he was so pleased to be involved in that, his little eyes shone with the wonder of it all.

After we'd done all of that, I'd hoped we could stay a bit longer. Elizabeth would usually fall asleep in the noisiest of places, but not that night. I walked her up and down the road in the stroller; Amelia tried, but Elizabeth wouldn't settle. It got to the point where I just said to the friend we'd had a lift with, 'Let's head back to yours. It's getting late and she won't sleep. Shall we call a taxi?'

Everyone said, 'No, it really isn't far! It's quicker than in the car.' They all said we'd need torches though as it was dark. We got sorted with those as they kept reassuring me it wasn't far. I got Elizabeth settled yet again in her stroller then . . .

It's all hazy.

It's all so very hazy.

Chapter Seven

The Incident

It was dark. The walk was dark.

It started to brighten a bit and I think that's because we were near some streetlights. I've been told since that we were singing '500 Miles.' That wouldn't surprise me, it would make perfect sense actually because we sang it a lot.

There was a bang.

Then there was a scream.

Two screams.

Three screams.

Just screams.

I don't think there will be a moment when I'll not hear those screams. They're always there, waiting for me. They came from my friend's children. I saw her and her kids standing in the central reservation of the road, and her partner was shouting at them. 'Take the kids home! Take the kids!'

I was holding onto the stroller with Elizabeth in it, but my friend took her from me.

I looked ahead and there was Fraser, lying on the ground.

I looked left, and some way away, was Stuey, also lying on the ground.

There was nothing else. I couldn't see a car; there was nothing other than two bodies, stretched far apart.

In my head, I was running between the two of them. That's what I remembered for so long. I didn't know who I should be with. For years, I wondered why I did that. I struggled with it. I struggled with why I didn't stay with my son. Why did I waste time running between them and therefore not helping either? I later found out that never happened. I later found out that I'd stayed with Fraser throughout while some other people were with Stu.

I do remember yelling, 'Please! Please take care of my husband! Please look after him!'

My friend's partner was attempting CPR and Fraser was making this strange noise.

The noise – the noise of my baby trying to breathe, trying so hard.

My friend's partner started talking to him about football, trying to keep him with us. He kept telling him about Liverpool and I was thinking, *'But he's not a Liverpool fan.'* The noise, the wheeze, the clicking whistle, was coming from my Fraser all the time. I felt I'd been sucked up and put in the middle of a movie set and there was someone I loved in the heart of it, right in front of me and I didn't know what their script was. You could never imagine this; no one could ever have this as a scenario in their mind. I felt disconnected and yet deep in the horror of it all.

They were so far apart. How had that happened? No – there was a question before that - what had happened? What had made them so far apart? It was a deserted road and somehow my husband and my little boy had been picked up and flung onto different parts of it. There were two people lying on the road and they were my husband and my son, and none of this was real. It couldn't be. We'd been at a party. Stu had been Father Christmas. Fraser had been hugging me all night. Elizabeth was in her stroller. Those were the facts, not this.

Time just stopped.

It felt like forever until an ambulance arrived, and I can't tell you what was happening until it got there. I don't even know if I was holding Fraser. I think he was on my friend's partner's lap, and I was at the side. But I don't know. I don't know. It was as if I had died, and I was overlooking them. I was up above them, watching, and none of it could be real, could it?

A jump.

The next moment, my friend's sister and her brother-in-law turned up.

Another jump.

I was in a police car.

Another jump.

I was now at the hospital, the Royal Glamorgan.

My brain had stopped functioning and so had parts of my memory.

I was in a waiting room.

My phone was completely out of charge. I couldn't call anyone, so a police officer asked for details of my parents while I was in the waiting room with my friend's partner, her sister, and her brother-in-law. There was a nurse; there was definitely a nurse.

Another jump.

Mum and Dad were there.

'I'm so sorry it's taken so long to get here,' Mum said as she held me. What did she mean? It had been seconds since I'd been in the road looking at Stu and Fraser, just seconds. 'Dad got the call and drove to your house as he wasn't sure what had happened, then the road to here was closed because of . . .'

Because of what?

Because of what had happened to my family. Because a car had hit Stu, had hit Fraser, and resulted in us all being here.

Another jump.

Someone was there, someone was talking to me. But she was saying something that didn't make sense at all.

'I'm so sorry. I'm so sorry.'

What was she sorry for?

'I'm just so very sorry.'

Why did she keep saying that? I had no idea who she was. Why was she sorry for something and why was she telling me about it?

'Your husband. He didn't make it. He's passed away. You need to say goodbye, Anna-Louise.'

They said that nicely, I know that. They were telling me to say goodbye to Stuey. And that was because he wasn't here any longer. And someone – the same someone? – said it again.

'You need to say goodbye to him, Anna-Louise.'

In reality, they were getting me to identify the body.

Another jump.

There was Stu. Just lying on a hospital bed and there wasn't a mark on him; he looked perfect. I sat with him, I know that, and I know that I held his hand, but I didn't think he was dead. Not really. It had all been too quick, it just wasn't something that could have happened, could it? It had only been a few seconds since we'd all been walking together. I sort of wondered how we'd even got here – and I sort of wondered when it would all turn real again.

Somebody turned to me, maybe the nurse, and said, 'What would Stu wish in relation to organ donation?'

'Oh, I know this,' I answered immediately. 'Yes. Consent. Everything.'

That was why he'd told me, I thought. That was why he'd wanted to talk so much after the Pride of Britain Awards.

Another jump.

I was sitting with Fraser alone. I felt like I was in something like a corridor. It was the middle of a huge, dark room with lots of machines, but it felt like it was just us. I started to talk to him. There were so many monitors on my Bear and one was checking his blood pressure.

'It's extremely low,' a doctor said. 'His blood pressure – we're very concerned, Anna-Louise.'

I was holding my boy's hand and just watching these numbers. Instinctively, I started to talk to him, like my friend's partner did at the scene, about football. It came from somewhere, nowhere.

'Fraser's got the ball! Fraser's running! Fraser's shooting! Fraser scores!' I said it over and over and over again, and every time I did, every time I told him he had scored a goal, his blood pressure went up. I kept talking, I kept saying it.

Another jump.

I wasn't with Fraser. I was in another room where my brother and sister were. Nothing more. Just the memory of the room.

Another jump.

There was a doctor standing beside me. 'Fraser is incredibly poorly, Anna-Louise. He's suffered major brain trauma. We're on the phone to the main brain trauma unit in Bristol to see if they have any advice as to how we deal with this level of injury. I'm afraid we don't think Fraser is going to make it.'

Another jump.

Where did they go? Where did people go so quickly when they had just been speaking to me seconds before? I was just bewildered. Mum said, 'Father Irving is away on holiday, but Father Philip is coming to see Stu for a blessing.'

Another jump.

Someone was talking again.

'It's our belief that Fraser is brain dead. We've spoken to the consultants at Bristol and there's nothing they or we can do.'

I broke down then.

'You've just taken away my husband! You can't take away my child as well. You can't! He's responding to me about football. You can't do this! You can't say this is all that can be done!' I fell to the floor and sobbed. Then I felt as if my whole body was shaking. I ran to the toilet next door and screamed and screamed. I've never cried like that in my life. My heart was pulled out of me as I fell to the floor and vomited.

I broke.

Another jump.

Someone had come back. 'We can't promise anything, but we've contacted the consultant at Bristol again about Fraser.'

'There's hope? There's a glimmer of hope?'

No one answered me.

A jump.

The consultants came from Bristol and said that they would need to relocate Fraser there by ambulance as soon as possible.

'I want to go with him,' I told the doctor. I would be allowed but I had to be in the front so that the medical team could be in the back with as much space as possible. Little did I realise that it was probably in case they needed to resuscitate him again. I now know that not only was Fraser resuscitated at the side of the road just after the car hit him, but he was also resuscitated on the ward. I had to sign what seemed like a million forms to release him for that trip to Bristol. I didn't care; it was that glimmer of the light that mattered, that they weren't just writing my baby off.

I recall the ambulance driver was called Steve. I thought about how I had met Stuey through our own Steve in Dublin and that he was now Elizabeth's godfather. Somehow, it felt as if we were safe at that point.

Before we left the Royal Glamorgan Hospital, Steve was approached by another paramedic, and they discussed the route they had to take to Bristol. Once the discussion was settled, Steve reluctantly told me that he had no option but to drive down THAT road, the same road that I had just witnessed my baby boy being hit.

We left the Royal Glamorgan Hospital and I never took my eyes off Fraser for nearly the whole trip. I looked over my shoulder at my baby lying there in the back and just stared at him. It was light by then, but I couldn't understand how that could be as I felt everything had happened in a few minutes.

We had to drive down that road. The road where it all happened. As we passed the spot, it was now daylight. It was bright, it was airy, and it was so busy; so much of a different feeling from the eerie dark street the night before. I closed my eyes as if that would escape my pain as we approached; like shutting your eyes on a roller coaster but it made it dark again like the night before and all I could hear was my bear's gurgling noises. It was the only moment I didn't look at Fraser for the whole trip.

That ambulance journey was peaceful. Strangely peaceful. It was calm. There was no sense in watching the monitors as I'd done on the ward. There was just a sense that this was a journey we had to do.

Another jump.

Fraser was taken into a private ward when we got to Bristol. It was clean and bright, so different to the dark hospital ward where he'd been and now it was all so white.

It was like Heaven.

My little boy didn't look sick. He looked perfect, not ill. I couldn't see a mark on him. He was my angel.

We were given a private waiting room.

Another jump.

The tiny waiting room was full – Stu's parents, my sister's husband, Mum, more people, I think. We were away from Fraser in there, but we could all go and see him on our own. I'd go and then come back to that room, but I don't know why I was moving about. I don't know why I didn't sit permanently next to Fraser on the ward. Was I told to move? Were they doing tests? I have no idea.

Another jump.

Father Irving turned up. He'd been on holiday like Mum had said, but he was here now. He was vaping and I said to him, 'You can't do that in a hospital!'

'What are they going to do? Chuck out a clergyman?'

That couldn't have been the first thing we said to each other, but it's the only thing I remember.

Another jump.

I remember ringing a friend and saying, 'Gosh, this is pants. It's really pants.'

She said, 'I know you don't like swearing but I think you can say this is a little bit worse than pants, Spanna.'

'It's pants, it's just pants,' I repeated.

Another jump.

I was getting messages from people. Somehow my phone was charged. People had read online that Fraser was dead - the BBC had reported that. I felt that I had to go on social media to let everyone know he was not, that he was not dead. He was still alive, and I needed everyone to pray for him.

Another jump.

Father Irving blessed Fraser and then . . . we looked at my peaceful, calm boy and Father Irving said to me, 'You do realise

Span, he's no longer there? His body is there but Fraser is no longer there.'

I looked at him and said, 'I think so. I think I know.'

He wasn't going to make it.

My Fraser Bear wasn't going to make it.

Chapter Eight

Fraser Passes

When I was in that room, someone phoned me to ask about tissue donation for Stu – there were a lot of 'someones' during all of it. It didn't click with me at the time, but not much could be 'utilised' of Stu as he'd died at the scene. When I'd said 'yes', I thought that was it. We now had opt-out in Wales, and he'd even opted in; it seemed clear cut and I just assumed they would proceed but so many questions had to be asked and all of them were directed at me. They must have known what was going on with Fraser and all I could say was, 'I won't answer these questions now as I think I might be completing two questionnaires very soon.'

I don't know where that sentence came from but it's what I told them. What was the point of answering now when there would potentially be so much more to answer shortly? I didn't really understand that things weren't being processed with Stu because I hadn't answered the questions.

Everything was on hold. As far as I was concerned, I had answered the one query and that was it.

The consultant came in and she said, 'I'm afraid that we do think Fraser is brain dead. Obviously, there are tests we can undertake for you to confirm that, but I believe that they'll confirm what we believe too. Have you thought about whether you would like to donate any of Fraser's organs?'

At once, all of us in the room said 'Yes.'

We all said it at the same time.

Wait.

Did that happen? It's another thing I'm not sure about. My memory doesn't know. Maybe I said 'yes' and everyone nodded. Maybe everyone kept quiet and waited to see how I'd respond. I don't know, I honestly don't know. It felt like the whole room answered, but maybe it was that everyone knew.

'We'll get a specialist nurse here for you who deals with organ donation.'

I understood the tests they were going to do given my experience with medical ethics and the law. There is a test – the brain stem death test – with certain medical parameters that have to be met for someone to be declared brain dead. I recalled one of the questions we'd debated was whether the test caused pain to the person, but if you're brain dead, you shouldn't be feeling any pain anyway. I knew what the test was, and I knew it was lengthy. I asked whether I could do the questionnaire for donation while the tests were being undertaken, then we would be ready to go if Fraser satisfied the test. I think that was me trying to utilise the time, trying to be efficient in the middle of hell.

They rang the specialist nurse – bearing in mind it was a Sunday – and everything started to fall into place. We'd had the medical professional conversation but then Father Irving said to me, 'Let's all go and see Fraser now.' It was really a little goodbye service for my boy, a sort of last rites at the bedside.

I think that Dad and Father Irving were hoping that would be enough for me, but how could I just walk away and never see him again, never touch him again, never speak to him again? I sent everyone but Dad away while I answered all of the questions, but I couldn't stop going in and out, in and out, to my baby. He was still there; he was still breathing. He might not have been living, but he was still breathing. I needed to fill myself up on him as I'd never have the opportunity again. How could I possibly get to the point where I'd think I'd had enough?

I know that I've never had much sense of time, but I can promise you that answering those questions for donation took what seemed like forever, at least two hours. The organ donation nurse kept leaving the room, taking calls, coming back in, leaving again, coming back in, until my dad said, 'You have to come in, stay and finish this – otherwise I'm taking my daughter home. She's been through almost 24 hours of hell; you need to get this done.' Every time that the donation nurse went out, I returned to Fraser.

LIFE: A STORY OF BELIEVING

They'd quickly told me that the tests had confirmed what I knew – he was brain dead, but they needed to keep him breathing for the organ donation.

He was there. But gone.

The questions for Stu were fine. I could fly through them as he'd shared everything with me, he'd always been open. I knew he'd never been bitten by a bat, I knew where he had travelled, I knew his sexual practices, I knew the answers to all of the questions. It was a very procedural approach to his life and such a difficult process to go through after such trauma.

I spoke to the consultant and also telephoned Jess. Something flashed in my memory and I recalled that she had her son's heartbeat from before she donated his kidney. I wanted that. I asked how she had done it and organised, in that middle period, to get Fraser's heartbeat recorded.

Little did I realise his heart would be donated.

You go through the list of organs you will give, but I didn't comprehend how poignant his heart would be in relation to what was going to happen later. I wanted to have that heartbeat, I needed to have it. There are obvious things that happen when a parent loses a child, when you lose a loved one. Handprints are taken, maybe footprints. I have them somewhere, but those things can suffer wear and tear over time, those things that are meant to be a lasting memory. But I wanted something more. I wanted to be able to hear Fraser's heart, maybe not today, maybe not tomorrow, but I knew I would need it at some point. Jess was actually trying to help behind the scenes with her organ donation nurse in Wales but I had no idea the extent of what was going on. I was emotionally exhausted. My stomach was in bits, and they did give me some medication for that, but I can't remember overly crying, not the way I had in Wales.

We left Bristol at 10 pm that night. My brother came and picked us up - we were going back to Mum and Dad's house. It was pitch dark as I watched the motorway lights from the back seat. I felt like the world was so quiet, so surreal. Time had stopped yet again. I didn't want that journey to end. I wanted to stay in that car; it felt safe.

Another jump.

We arrived at Mum and Dad's house and I have no idea what happened in the aftermath of my arrival there. I know we all sat around the table and I know that Elizabeth was in the double bed where I would eventually sleep, but at that point, I hadn't slept for over forty hours.

On the Monday morning, a GP from my practice arrived at the house. She gave me some diazepam but I didn't take it. On the label, it said, 'Do not drink alcohol while taking this medication'. That scared me. If you weren't even meant to have one drink with these tablets, how on earth could I look after Elizabeth if I took them? I'd be in no fit state and she needed me more than ever. I couldn't take the luxury of being heavily medicated but I needed to talk to her; I needed to tell her what had happened to her Daddy and big brother. I stood in the sitting room, watching my three-year-old daughter playing without a care in the world. She had no idea and I wished she could stay like that forever. Her world had changed in an instant and I had to find a way to explain to her what had happened. Fraser had always been older than his years and now I needed Elizabeth to understand what had happened without worrying her. How on earth could I do that?

She smiled at me when I sat down beside her but kept playing. My eyes wandered to the window and I saw two birds on a branch. 'Elizabeth,' I began, 'do you see those two birds there? That's like Daddy and Fraser now. Daddy and Fraser have died – they're like those birds. They're not coming back, but they'll always be watching us, just like them.'

That was it. That was all I could tell her.

She just said, 'OK,' and gave me a hug before continuing to play. She didn't cry, she didn't have any questions – she just accepted it.

I had been given a Family Liaison Officer who told me on the Monday, 'I just want you to be aware that there are some not very nice people out there. This will hit the press and you will get some really negative comments about the fact that you were walking across a road late at night with children.'

Instinctively, I thought, 'Am I to blame for all of this now? Should I have had Elizabeth in bed at 7 pm at night? Should we not have gone to a friend's party?' I knew the answer was 'no'; I knew that was what people did at Christmas time, but he put that doubt in my mind. The blame versus culpability thing was really hard and the moment the FLO said that my immediate thoughts were, 'What's coming? What am I going to be hit with?'

I couldn't deal with people outside of me. I didn't think anyone could blame me more than I did, but the thought that someone would make the effort to do that made me want to throw up. I was to blame – if someone else said it, then I was to blame, or Stu was. I couldn't have his memory of how good he was tarnished by that. Were people going to say that my son was to blame? The FLO's words did scare me.

It was such a busy house and there was an endless stream of visitors. I was only focused on one thing. When I'd left the hospital, they said they would call to explain about Fraser's operation. All I can remember is watching my phone constantly, no matter who was around me, no matter what was going on. I just wanted that phone to ring. I didn't understand the complexities of the operation Fraser would be undergoing or even the importance of it really. I just wanted to hear about him, I wanted someone to tell me how my baby was.

That was strange I suppose as I knew he was brain dead; I knew in my head that he was no longer here but in my soul, I had left him with his heart still beating. That's always been the hardest thing. I actually left my child while his heart was still beating, while he was still breathing. I just needed them to call and let me know what my Fraser Bear was like now.

I just sat there, watching that phone, wanting it to ring, wanting to know how he was.

I now know how difficult that operation was; it would have been such a major endeavour. None of that was in my mind. They didn't ring until late afternoon. At least, that's when I think it was.

'The operation was a success,' I was told.

'A success?' A success. The word you want to hear after a loved one has had an operation, but in this case, what? What did it mean for my boy? How could it be a 'success'?

'Yes, it went well.'

'OK – what happened?'

'Well, we were very respectful of Fraser,' the woman told me. 'He was given a guard of honour going into theatre – and a minute's silence.'

I can't remember whether he got that before or after. Those tiny gestures for a little boy who should never have been there in the first place. All I could think was, he'd rather have had a minute's clapping or cheering, he'd rather have had noise. He wasn't a quiet little boy after all.

I went through it twice really. Bear left me twice. I broke my heart as I thought about how the hardest thing had been walking away from him still breathing, his heart still beating, but now he was gone in another way too. He'd gone again.

When we were going through all the organ donation process, I'd been going back and forth constantly, I felt I needed to do that. When I got that phone call, because he was no longer breathing, it was the first step towards acceptance that there was no choice for me now. Up until that point, as a mother, it is all your choice – you can say whether you want organ donation to go ahead or not. Fraser had also responded to me at the Royal Glam. I knew he wasn't braindead then in Wales but once in Bristol, I could see what the medics did. I knew in my head, I'd studied the braindead stem test; I knew he wasn't there. Father Irving had told me, but it still doesn't stop that niggle as a parent as to whether you could have done more.

Could he have been that miracle?

Could God have stepped in?

Maybe I should have had hope.

I now think that maybe, the fact that he survived that trip to Bristol was Fraser's miracle. If he hadn't managed to do that, then he could never have donated, he would have died in vain. He gave me that.

That call to say his soul was no longer was a relief, but it also meant losing him again. The worst thing was, now my son was on his own. He'd been surrounded by medical staff since the moment he arrived in hospital, and now? No one. He was alone in Bristol, and it hit me – where's Stu? What happens now? Can I get them together?

My next fight would be to achieve that. I had to make sure one of us was with Fraser. I knew it was just their bodies, but I needed it.

Another jump.

Matt, the police officer came back (maybe he'd never been away, I wouldn't have known) to try and explain some more about what was happening. 'There is an ongoing investigation,' he told me.

'About the accident?' I asked.

'The incident,' he corrected me.

I had no reason in my head at that point to believe that there was any reason for what had happened or that anyone was to blame. My recollections of the road were just that they'd been hit by a car, but I hadn't seen any cars there; I hadn't seen a vehicle. I couldn't recall if there was someone staggering around or being bundled into a police car. I couldn't even remember the road that well.

Father Irving and my brother had both said at one point, 'I feel for the driver as well.' I'd agreed. 'Can you imagine how to live with that? Two people dying from that collision. It must be awful for them.'

Matt did tell me that someone had stopped further down the road but that was all I knew. This young man had been going to collect someone from a Christmas party, and I wondered if he'd been driving too fast. But then, Stu was a horror for driving too fast and I just thought it was an accident. It was an 'incident' though as Matt said, although I still struggle to call it that. They'd held onto

Stu's phone – I have no idea why as he was the one crossing a road, how could he have been to blame in any way?

Matt was now my Family Liaison Officer, but my sister Bridget was effectively my police liaison person. Everything went through her and she decided what to tell me. I couldn't understand why the house phone kept ringing, and why there were constant knocks at the door. It didn't seem to stop, there was a constant stream of people outside.

'It's the media,' Bridget told me. 'They know what happened – the story's everywhere.'

Matt had to put a note up in the porch to say, '*This property is not to be approached by anyone in the media.*'

Then the grief tourists started to appear – a school friend from years ago, people I hadn't even spoken to in so long; they all arrived. People expected to come in, they thought the doors would just be open to them and they could insert themselves into my grief. It was a bizarre situation. The kitchen was full of the mums of Fraser's friends at one point, and I felt as if there was a hierarchy being established, a fight to be the alpha mother, trying to get control in that group of people. I think people were trying to be supportive, but they also seemed to be deciding amongst themselves who had more of a right to be upset or to be near to me. It was exhausting. Trying to deal with the different social behaviours of those who had just parachuted in and expected me to engage with them, almost on a social level, was bewildering.

This was my life now; this was all I could see ahead of me. Loss and heartache and a strange, but perfectly understandable, sense that none of it was real.

Chapter Nine

A Shrine

I find it almost impossible to put everything together from those early days because so much was happening. I think of one thing, then I remember something else. I go back to what the police were saying and then wonder what stage that was. I recall some words from Father Irving but then think that he perhaps said them to me weeks later but I have mixed them up with other discussions.

Grief isn't linear. Of course, you can put dates on the main events, on the day we went to the Christmas parties, on the early hours when it all happened, on the day I left hospital, all of that is recorded – but the other bits? They're all over the place. They come and go, they are snippets and snatches of things; they are memories you try to grab like dissipating dreams that rush off from your consciousness as soon as your eyes open in the morning. You think you thought something or said something, or saw something, or remembered something - but you also don't know what's real anymore; you don't know what comes where or when.

I became aware, very quickly, of how much I was going to need my family to get me through, as they'd done at the hospital. However, they were going through this trauma too. They'd lost a son, a son-in-law, a grandson, a brother, a nephew, a best friend, an uncle, and they were trying to support their daughter, their sister, when all they could see was pain. How would they get the strength to do that? For the first couple of days, when the people who were important in our lives were ringing or popping over, I tried to give them some responsibility for the others. For example, I asked a friend if she would keep checking on Bridget. My sister needed to look after me and yet she needed looking after, she needed someone to go to and talk to. Everyone else needed to be cared for or they'd be unable to be there for me.

I often thought it must have been harder for them to deal with me than it was for me to deal with it. You can't control people, places, or things, but you can control your reactions and emotions. Sometimes I do think it's easier to be me. Yes, I'm the one who's suffering but I don't know how I would deal with seeing that pain in someone that I loved so much. It's easier for me to have the pain.

Another jump.

'I'm really sorry,' Matt said to me, 'but people are attending the scene of the incident in order to lay flowers in tribute.'

'That's alright,' I told him.

'It's dangerous I'm afraid. We're worried there might be an accident.' *Another accident*, I wanted to say as it was still that to me, not an incident, but I knew there was a difference in legal terms no matter what my heart told me. 'Can you think of somewhere else that people might be able to leave flowers?'

'The park, I suppose, the park next to our house. The boys played football there.'

Another jump.

'Do you want to go and visit the park?' someone asked me. I have no idea who it was. I don't even know if it was Monday or Tuesday.

I dragged myself there and I saw that it had already begun. Flowers, teddies, football shirts, 'Tangfastics' for Stu as they were his favourite sweets, all these little things that were associated with my boys. The entire place was full. It hit me that this was such a big thing for so many people – and there was me right in the middle of it, treading water, trying to process what was actually happening.

From that point, we couldn't put the news on as the lead story was my boys, my loss. I had every newspaper trying to contact me. When Stu's parents left to go and get me some clothes from my house, they were followed by the press to try and get quotes. It was like some horrific paparazzi nightmare. There was a massive shrine in the park, there were journalists everywhere; people were crying, everyone wanted a part of me. Some of those people still say they remember where they were when they heard about Stu and Fraser. I don't know why they think it's appropriate to say that, to make

LIFE: A STORY OF BELIEVING

me share in what their memories are. I don't want their story of it - I have my own.

I never stop them. I can't do that. They think they're being helpful by telling me of the impact on them, but it doesn't help, it doesn't help at all. Why would I need to know how upset they were when they found out given that I was at Fraser's bedside trying to compute everything, trying to fathom my loss? Why would I need to know how much they'd cried when I was drained of tears?

I feel it was almost beyond me to see the sheer mass of what people had left at the shrine and to think 'that's for my boys'. My boys who I'd lost forever - that was all for them. I don't think I had it in my mind that I'd never see them again, even though I'd just had that conversation with Elizabeth. I didn't understand it myself. I wanted to make them proud and make sure I did everything right because they were so special and important. The more I saw the public displays, I realised it was an affirmation that they were that special and important; I wasn't the only one who thought that way. Eventually, I realised just how many people we'd crossed paths with. Everybody knows everybody in Cardiff but we really had come across so many people in our lives. I'd gone to a really big local comprehensive school where everyone knew me as Head Girl. I'd also gone to university in Cardiff, I'd had a part-time job in a chemist for fourteen years, and Dad had his own printing business, that had employed over a hundred people. In addition, I'd had three law practices, we knew everyone at Church, I'd run Slimming

World all over the city, Stu worked in a massive company, we had cycling friends, we'd known hundreds through music, and there were all of our family connections and everyone knew. Cardiff seemed very small all of a sudden.

When the boys passed away, I had a multitude of questions about whether it might have been part of some kind of divine plan. Before they had died, there were so many things that I wondered whether God had set this all out for me, and that would evolve because He gave me the strength and the knowledge and the courage to be able to get through it – and do what I've done since.

LIFE: A STORY OF BELIEVING

Father Irving said to me, 'It would never be part of God's plan to cause you pain.' Those words helped but I still had questions. Why did I give blood a few weeks before? Why did Stu raise this discussion about organ donation a few weeks before? Why, the night that it happened, would Fraser not leave my side? It just felt like I would be better equipped to be able to deal with all of that if there was some sort of purpose. I never really questioned my faith as such though. I am still a believer, but those questions were there, that's for sure. It felt like a dream, it felt like I was playing out a part in a movie and all of a sudden, it would go back to how it was. Nothing felt like I was living. I was utterly exhausted, but I had so much to do, and it all had to be perfect. I had to do it right for Stu and Fraser. I couldn't just go to bed and hide.

'What if we'd just got a taxi?' I wept to my brother. 'What if we'd just got a taxi?'

'What if you'd never gone to Dublin?' he gently replied. 'What if you'd never met or had the life you had?'

He'll never know how important those words were at that time.

Stu had been through a really bad cycling accident when Elizabeth was only just turned one and broken his collarbones. His helmet was split right down the middle and if he hadn't been wearing it, he would have died. That could have been the moment but it wasn't. I'd been blessed with another two years with him, and I tried to hold onto that. Grief makes you think such strange things and you grasp for consolation – this was one of mine. He'd almost died then but I got to keep him for a bit longer.

I went to the park at one point and there was a boy with his mum. He was a couple of years older than Fraser and I think he had some difficulty with emotions and how to express them. He came right up to me and said, 'Ha ha, your son's dead and his dad too, they're not coming back!' That will stay with me forever.

Those words were like a stab in the heart. Apart from that, it was all surreal. Not his words though, not his words. Those hit me like a brick wall but the fact that he was right, wasn't he? They were never coming back. I think I still have difficulty in accepting this.

I was speaking to the police a lot at that time, and given that Fraser's operation had been completed, I could only wonder, what now? An undertaker came within the first couple of days but we couldn't formalise anything because we didn't know when the Coroner's Report would come in for the Crown Prosecution Service, or even where it would all take place. Fraser was in Bristol, Stu was in the Royal Glam, our hospital was in Cardiff. I eventually got them both into the Coroner's Office in Cardiff, I got them together, but it was a fight. I felt a little bit of strength that Stu had passed away first because that meant he would be there, waiting, to look after Fraser, but I had nowhere to get my own strength. I was told that the investigations were ongoing into the driver and that he could ask for his own report to be undertaken. If that happened, it would be January before a funeral could take place.

I broke down at that point.

'Please God, please. Don't let him ask for that. I can't deal with all of this waiting until January,' I prayed.

Chapter Ten

Aftermath

When you lose someone you love, funeral arrangements become something you focus on. You get through knowing that you have all of this to do, and that once it's over, you can fully open yourself up to whatever is there. I didn't have that point in mind as I had no idea when the funerals would happen; it was completely out of my hands.

'Why don't we open the church on Saturday?' Father Irving said. 'I'll open it all day for people to come and pay their respects.' He'd been with me all of the time anyway, but he knew people had to grieve and reflect and I think he needed that too. As soon as he said it, I realised that I wanted it as a symbol of coming home again. St Martins had always been in my life and now it would be there for me once more.

The same day, Jess arrived. I'd been speaking to her at the hospital – she was the mum of Teddy – when I was desperate to get Fraser's heartbeat captured. Bless her, she'd gone to Build-a-Bear and got teddies for me and Elizabeth with my little boy's heartbeat inside.

She was working with 2 Wish Upon A Star at the time. 'Look, I hope you don't mind, but we were proposing to do a balloon release on Saturday where the shrine is, for the children to remember Fraser. Is that OK?'

Obviously, I agreed.

On the Wednesday, I got a call from the Organ Donation people who said that they would like to come out and see me so that they could advise about Fraser's donations. I was presented with a letter to tell me what organs had been retrieved and where they had gone. Fraser's heart, his beautiful, precious heart, had gone to a baby boy. His lungs had gone to another child. His kidney and liver to a little girl, and his other kidney to a lady in her 30s. That's all you're told; that's all you're given. Such a little list for a big life.

The Organ Donation Service realised the magnitude of the media attention that surrounded us at that point and said they would send someone from their Communications Department later that week to do an interview with me. This would ensure that the correct information was fed out. I was already getting really frustrated by the coverage as they had said Fraser was dead whilst I sat at his bedside in hospital. Not only was this hurtful but it gave such misleading 'facts' about the process. He couldn't have been gone at that point or the donations wouldn't have been an option. An American paper said that I'd been the one to switch

Fraser's heart monitor off as I guess that gave them the dramatic image they needed, irrespective of how much it hurt me. I jumped at the chance to speak to someone who was medically aware of what had happened and who could deal with all of that. It took hours but at least it meant they would be the ones dealing with the national press. I gave them lots of pictures that I wanted to be used, thinking that my social media was protected and secure, but somehow the media got access to everything when the story hit that weekend, everything on my personal page through a public work account. I had no idea that could be done but it resulted in them using photographs of the boys that really weren't how I wanted to remember them.

That weekend, the balloon release was also going on, the church was open, and I went to both. The church was there for people to quietly reflect whenever they wanted but I wish there had been a Book of Remembrance, something I could look back on now and show Elizabeth. Cardiff City also did a two-minute round of applause in memory of Stu and Fraser, and my brother went to that for me. People were trying to be kind but there was just so much – the church, the balloon release, the football match, a bike ride of 200 people, the police, trying to get the boys together, Elizabeth, the media, everything – I had no space to grieve and, although it might sound awful, I was jealous of anyone who did have that.

LIFE: A STORY OF BELIEVING

I was constantly wondering what was right and what I'd made up – what had actually happened and what hadn't happened. I'd been told by Matt on the Monday that I wasn't to talk to anyone about events as it was an ongoing investigation, and I'd have to give evidence and make a statement after the funeral. That meant I had no one to talk it out with. I don't think I was feeling; I don't think I was doing. I knew that I would have to go back to what had happened that night at some point. Nobody else in mine or Stu's family should have to do that or know the things that had occurred. Maybe that was unfair as they didn't understand fully what had happened, but I wasn't allowed to talk about it, so what choice did I have? I asked if Father Irving would sit in on my police interview so that I didn't have to have a family member hear it all. Maybe it wasn't the nicest thing I'd asked my parish priest to experience with me, but in my head, it was like confession. He was used to listening to things and I knew he would hold my hand and make sure I was alright. I decided to park it in one part of my brain and deal with the immediate. I'd process the questions as they came in and the emotions as they arrived too. Every night I prayed. Every night I talked to the boys.

I remember hugging the Fraser Bears I was given from such an early point. Elizabeth was always hugging hers too. Other than the contact I had from that, I couldn't allow myself to feel, because I was scared that if I fell, I'd never get up again. If that happened, I wouldn't be able to do them proud; I wouldn't be able to deal with everything that I had to deal with. It was definitely a matter of fight or flight and I had the biggest ever fight on my hands. I didn't comprehend how much I was battling though. I should have allowed a bit of flight in there, I should have broken down. I should have allowed something to come through. From that point, it became harder and harder and harder, and continues to be hard, to ask for help. The fight kicked in so hard, as my protector, and I'm not sure it's ever left. I wanted to make sure this was as easy on everybody else as possible but who knows how much of me was lost in the process? I have no idea and sometimes I feel as if no one cares enough to find out anymore.

Everything had to be right for my bears, for Stu and Fraser, but I also didn't want anyone else to feel they had to do more than they could cope with. I welcomed their assistance but ultimately, every decision had to come down to me - the type of coffin, whether something went ahead, what was in or not in the funeral, funeral cars, what was I going to put them in clothing wise - these weren't decisions that anyone else could make. It was all for me to decide but I'm also very glad in a strange way that was the case as otherwise I would have had input that wasn't welcome. My family was so supportive but they were also very respectful. I got to make all of the decisions. It was always up to me. I chose every single thing in the funeral. I got them back together; there was no one interfering.

One thing that was hard was that Stu and Fraser seemed to be lumped together as one – as one loss, as one tragedy. That might have been the hardest aspect of all. That affected how I interacted with them too. If I was talking to one, I felt guilty that I wasn't talking to the other. I'd be crying for the loss of my husband and feeling guilty that I wasn't crying for my son. I'd be wanting my son to be there for the biggest hug in the world, but why wasn't I wanting my husband as well? That's still there and I don't think it will ever go.

I spoke a lot to people and it was lovely to hear their stories about Stu and Fraser, but when I went to bed, I was alone. Yes, Elizabeth was there, but I was back in my childhood bedroom and almost regressing. I'd cry but had to keep it quiet unless it upset Elizabeth. Help me, guide me, show me, I would ask the boys. I never asked God to look after them as it was a given they'd be in Heaven as they were angels. The hardest thing was definitely to make all of these decisions without having Stu there. He wasn't around to help with the loss of Fraser and he was the only other person who would understand that.

The ways in which my grief presented were completely unpredictable. I now know that the unpredictability is the only thing which is predictable. I went from sometimes being really angry about the times Stu had been with Fraser - why hadn't I got him all the time? – to getting angry with myself for having that anger in the first place. I never blamed Stu, I couldn't allow that to go into myself, and that's why I never blamed the driver at the beginning because if you're going to say someone is culpable, who is most guilty? Is it the driver? Is it us for crossing that road? Is it Stu for not seeing the car? Is it me for convincing him not to take the car that night? I never blamed anyone who was outside of those people, but part of the problem was I couldn't talk about it to anyone as I was a witness, and their minds were probably going into overdrive trying to work out what had happened. Maybe they thought I was blaming them, which I never would.

I just wanted help from Stu.

I had no idea how to deal with my grief while dealing with everyone else's. Instead of recognising and realising that I could have fallen apart or relied on someone, things then wouldn't have happened the way that they did. I don't know what would have been for the 'best', I really don't. Those moments were just frozen and the hardest thing now is that I've never dealt with those weeks, those months afterwards. I was just on that treadmill. I couldn't get off. Every day there was a question, every day there was something that needed doing, every day there was some action I had to take.

People would try and do things, get me out of the house for half an hour. Stu's boss, Ian, took me for lunch one day at Sainsbury's. All I did was try to make him feel better for that whole hour. I used to say to people, 'Don't hug me – don't be nice to me, because if you do that, I think I'll go. And there's no way back. Just let me keep focussed.'

I was going to have to wait so long to give my statement and I wasn't allowed to talk to anyone about what I'd witnessed. Even now, I question what I remember. Even knowing the legal side, the reliability of legal statements and what people think they remember didn't help. People want to fill in the gaps; they aren't being malicious, it's just a natural human response. I was more scared about remembering something that might make someone culpable, I didn't want anyone to be at fault, I just wanted it to be an accident.

I also had to deal with social media. You don't think you'll look. Everyone says ignore the Twitter trolls, or ignore the negativity, but it's some kind of sick pull that you can't help giving into, especially when you're lying awake every hour of the night. I did like those nights though as they were just me and listening to Elizabeth breathe at the side, to think and quietly cry, but I did read the posts at that time too. There were two that I'll always remember. They weren't even people trying to be awful, but the words stick with me. One mother said, *You are so brave for cutting up your dead son.* Until that moment, I hadn't thought of Fraser's donation as 'cutting him up.' I found that one terrible. The other one that sticks with me was, *I can't believe this has happened to such a beautiful family.* Why not? If we hadn't been their idea of a beautiful family, would we not deserve support? If we weren't the sort of picture that you could judge as 'normal' straightaway, would we have been less deserving? I struggled with that. Fraser and Stu were beautiful on the inside, I wanted them to be remembered for their good hearts and their love, not some instant judgement that they were the 'right sort' of people.

I had made a post before I left hospital about the hardest goodbye and doing it without Stu. Reading that now when I haven't for over six years brings back how alone I was. I never processed that; I was just within my own world. It brings it back in an instant.

The media jumped on us straight away, but when I went to Sainsbury's with Ian that day, I saw that it was Christmas. I'd forgotten. The boys loved Christmas. We always put our trees up on the first of the month as it was our wedding anniversary the next day, so we had a month of celebration. In the shop, there were carol singers, Christmas music on, people buying presents – and I was trying to get my boys back together at the Coroner's Office.

Life was going on. I wanted to cancel Christmas but I couldn't, especially not with a three-year-old. I don't think she would have known if I had, but I couldn't do that to her. I was putting on my brave face and dealing with everything that was coming through and I was getting comments like, 'Oh, you have to stay strong for Elizabeth.' That's not really helpful – that was exactly what I was doing. I had to be there for her, I couldn't let her down, and if anyone thought I was doing anything else, then I can't imagine they have ever had to deal with loss in their lives. She was my world and I knew that I was hers.

But there was so much to get through. So very much.

Chapter Eleven

Believe is Born

There is another jump as I'm thinking about all of this, as I'm writing it all down. I try to maintain a timeline in my head but there was just so much of everything. And then it hits me – what I've forgotten. And it's massive. It's everything that came from it.

Around the Wednesday or maybe the Thursday, we had to start talking about a funeral but, as I've said, Matt emphasised that they didn't know when it could be as we'd have to wait on the coroner. We could look at a tentative date however, and confirm it later. We hoped the funeral would be the following Saturday but wouldn't know until mid-week. Father Irving and I had a discussion and decided it would probably be best to be on a Saturday as we knew there would be a lot of people who wanted to attend, and this would give them the best chance. Although nothing could be set in stone yet, having that day and date in mind at least gave me something to work with. It was a starting point.

'What are you going to do about the collection at the funeral?' Father Irving asked me. 'I assume it's going to be for 2Wish?' This was the charity set up by our friend Rhian to support those who had been affected by sudden death in young people and it was a charity we had supported, but to be honest, it was all overwhelming, even at that stage. Stu had been the driving force behind setting up a Just Giving page for a bike ride many of us had planned to do in May. He was the fundraising coordinator for everyone's page and they'd all been organised in advance so that people could get started on getting support in over six months or so. There was already £25,000 in donations there and the original plan had been for anything generated to go to 2 Wish Upon A Star.

I turned to Father Irving and said, 'There has already been so much money paid in. Rhian and I have chatted a lot and we both feel something is needed in relation to organ donation – that's where it needs to go.' I'd told Rhian about the difficulties I'd had in hospital and about how concerned I was for the support that was given afterwards. She'd said she was of the same opinion and was worried that now we were opt-out in Wales, how much bereavement support could feasibly be offered. I think everyone was under a misconception at the time of opt-out that, all of a sudden, there would be a million donations overnight.

It was actually a soft opt-out, meaning that the flood of expected donations didn't happen at all. The worries about harvested organs certainly never came to fruition, but there was still not the level of support that was needed – as I'd found out only too well. For me, I knew that the questions asked at the time and the horribly impersonal, standard letters that were going out to anyone in my position were probably only the tip of the iceberg. Resources were clearly stretched and it was absolutely unforgivable that people weren't getting what they needed at such a horrendous time in their lives. I'd had a specialist nurse who came to me to bring my letter but I knew that didn't happen for everyone as it would mean there were fewer people in the hospital giving support to the families going through it. Corners were being cut, resources weren't being developed appropriately, and something had to be done.

I said to Rhian that I would look into some sort of organ donation charity so that we could work together. I knew there wasn't that sort of thing in Wales but was sure there must be elsewhere in the UK. Looking back on it, I can hardly believe that I threw myself into that when I had only just lost my son and husband. It had been a matter of days since we'd all been together, since our lives had been full of love and fun as we prepared for another wonderful Christmas – and now? Well, I could barely even comprehend what 'now' was.

I did a lot of online searches when I couldn't sleep, which was every night, and at every other moment when I needed to be distracted. Whilst on the Charity Commission website, I gasped when I saw there had been a charity called 'Believe.'

Fraser's favourite film.

I dug a little deeper and found that it was no longer in existence. From the moment I thought of it, the moment I saw that name, I knew that it would be perfect for my vision of helping families around organ donation - *Believe*. The fact that the old one was now shelved was a sign. That was Fraser showing me this was what I needed to do.

This was it. If there hadn't been that sign, I don't know what I would have done – but there it was, and I could see a way forward. I told Father Irving what I had found, and what I wanted.

'That's great,' he said, 'but you need to make everybody clear on what they are donating to if they're giving money at the service. You cannot have any element of confusion whatsoever.' He was very transparent and very serious in his guidance, and he was absolutely right. Looking back, I can see that he was trying to tell me that there were some people who would want to trip me up on anything; this didn't really sink in at the time, but I've certainly seen examples of it since.

This was just days after the boys had died and I was now having to get my business head on. We needed a clear definition - *I* needed to do this right. I don't think that I chose to set the charity up, it just happened. It was this snowball that started and suddenly turned into a monumental force I couldn't stop, but it was all to do with the fact that I knew something needed to be done.

I chatted with Jess and we decided that the balloon release would be a good idea to tell everybody about Believe. That was where the money would go - anything raised - that was what it was all about. Steve was also there from Ireland, on his own without his family. Father Irving had urged me to organise a press release and, as Steve was a very eloquent person, I was grateful to hand all of that over to him.

'Can you write it and read it at the release?' I asked him. 'I don't know what kind of state I'll be in.'

It's only now that so many details are coming through to me, that I realise how many jumps in my memory there were. When you face loss of those you have loved, you have to put up a wall, you just can't get through without doing that. For some people, that means getting through to the funeral, then they tell themselves they'll deal with it. For some people, it's surviving the first year or getting to the first event that they would have celebrated. For others, it might be going on holiday without their loved one or moving house, it might be scattering the ashes, it might be seeing a commemorative rosebush flowering. Everyone makes their own deals, everyone makes their own boundaries. Now, writing this, I'm allowing so much to come through and I can see where my wall was and how it worked for me – in some ways at least.

On the Saturday, Bridget took me to church and there were people from many parts of my life in the sanctuary of the church which I appreciated. People were really respectful there, they didn't look to me to do anything for them and I felt very, very protected. Father Irving had blown up a picture of the boys after they had done a school project together, which he'd put at the front of the church. The doors were open, people came in and had some quiet time for reflection as the organist played. After the chaos of the last few days, there was suddenly an air of calm and peace.

I stayed for about half an hour; that was all I needed, and I also had to get to the balloon release. As I walked towards that event, there were people coming from every single direction. I could see Fraser's teachers, parents, and children; I could see other teachers and other parents and other children from Elizabeth's nursery; I could see people from Stu's work. There were balloons everywhere – orange and black for Fraser's Panthers football colours, and blue and white for Stu as they symbolised 2Wish, for which he had been very active. I think, to me, that balloon release was for Fraser though. It was loud and packed and intense and it felt like it was for him.

I knew there would be a PA and my friends asked what music I wanted when the balloons were released – it had to be *Forever Young*. That was what Bear sang constantly. I looked around and it wasn't just the amount of people I was struck by, it was the amount of film crews too. *I'm being watched*, I thought. Steve read out the statement as I stood with Elizabeth in my arms. It was as if nothing else mattered, I just sang along, on my own, in the loudest voice with the boys. I felt like I could feel Fraser there alongside me, singing it. I truly did have that sense that he was beside me.

There were lots of couples around. I could see my parents together too and it made me so aware that I didn't have *my* person beside me to help me through. There were thousands of people there. I was far from alone and Bridget was holding my hand, but I was looking around, looking for my husband to get me through. I could feel Fraser in my heart, but where was Stu?

A news crew came over. After all the inaccuracies in the press, I did feel I needed to say something that came from me, rather than through another person or a statement. I did but then a lot of the day went by in a haze.

Whilst all of this was happening, in the Cardiff City stadium they dedicated their match to the boys and even held a minute's round of applause. Martin went with his friend to represent us and it felt so humbling to have all of this dedication and love to the boys - my boys.

That night, I actually went to the local pub with friends of Stu who had come for the event. It was the first time I'd been able to be an adult and talk about him. It got me through half past midnight, that time when it had all happened. Having Stu's friends around me that evening stopped me from dwelling on it as we spoke about our wedding, and they distracted me with old stories. I was so emotionally drained due to the day I'd been through that I actually slept after a couple of glasses of red wine that night. When I woke up the following morning, there was *this time last week* ... I still have that. The winter months are horrendous for it; I'm a lot better in the summer that's for sure.

On the Sunday, I'd heard that some people from cycling clubs were going to ride to the park to lay flowers. That felt like it was for Stu, even though it was for both of them. It seemed like they'd had separate tributes and that helped me. I went to that with a friend, holding my big Fraser bear, which was with me from the moment I got it. I could hug it all the time for comfort. I knew the cyclists were coming to pay tribute but it just seemed like they would never stop once they started, once the flood of them began. I have no idea how many there were, but it felt endless. It was like a film on a loop that I thought would go on forever.

I couldn't go to church that Sunday. I was drained, and my mind kept flitting back to the knowledge of that day a week ago, when I'd been travelling to Bristol and spending my day in the hospital there with Fraser. I hadn't stopped for a week – I haven't stopped since but on that day, I had no idea what was to come. The mouse wheel never stops turning. If it does and I fall off, what will happen then?

I never rested.

I never drew breath.

When the boys passed, I immediately lost my fear of dying because I think it's harder to live. The moment they passed, I thought, *I'm not scared any more.* Obviously, I would be scared of leaving my daughter and I'm petrified about everyone else dying, but my own existence? No. I'm not worried. I wouldn't want Elizabeth to lose her mother after losing her father and brother, but, for me, there's no fear.

As the next week went on, I was trying to plan the funeral even though I didn't know whether it would happen. Father Irving, Bridget and Steve all stepped forward to help with the organisation and content of the 'maybe-funeral', while Martin tried to secure somewhere for the wake. We could see how many people this had affected but where on earth would we be able to find somewhere that would accommodate them all? There was also the media to deal with. How could I ensure the funeral was private? Our church was on a main road - how could people park? Buses would come; how would that work? How could any of these logistics be worked out, and where in the world would I find the strength to do it all?

I picked up my notebook and a pen and wrote a heading.

'The Funeral'.

Chapter Twelve

Plans

Stu had said for years that he wanted to be cremated, but I'd always wanted to be buried. I was really upset at one point during the planning of the funeral, and half-jokingly said that he got his wish as he went first. However, I knew that I wouldn't keep him from Fraser; they needed to be together forever. There was a crematorium in Thornhill but it was public, so anyone would have been able to turn up and I couldn't risk that. I couldn't risk the media there, taking photos of us all, and making a circus of it. It was almost like being in wedding mode. I needed the right people at the cremation, not those who just got there early for a day out.

I still didn't know when it would happen, I was just hoping. I was living every day, just praying, literally praying to God every day that it could happen, and that the driver wouldn't ask for his own report. I couldn't understand, even with my legal knowledge, why he would apply for one, but that was the law and there was nothing I could do. I had been told that the report had been done for the CPS, but I was still completely in the dark about whether it would need to be repeated. I had no control over any of it. Instead, I just had to try and hope for the best, which was the funeral of my son and husband. Isn't it strange to hope for a funeral? But I just needed to say goodbye and know they were at peace.

Things finally started to come together. Martin managed to secure Cardiff City football stadium for the wake as the team was playing away that weekend. We also decided to have a private cremation in Barry so that the media wouldn't know where it was being held. Hopefully it would give the family some privacy as we knew they would turn up if it was public, we knew that given the coverage already. I was nothing more than an interesting feature to them at that point, a grieving widow to photograph with a tearjerking headline above her face, and someone to rack up those clicks and likes on social media. To them, I was not a real person.

Everything was planned in the hope that it would happen. As a family, we separated tasks. My brother became the logistics man, my sister became the conduit between people, and Father Irving helped me plan the service. In the background, Martin had already started to think about the launch of the charity and had got someone to design the logo. We even had a collection of Fraser bears that had been donated by the House of Fraser. It was during the first week that Fraser's friends' mums had gone into the store to buy bears for his classmates, and the shop actually donated them instead. The charity development was going on in the background too, which was something positive to drive forward, but it was surreal how much was happening. One of Stu's old colleagues looked into trademarks and I was constantly coming up with ideas. Other people were chipping in too - all of those little things helped while I tried to crack on with the funeral arrangements, but I am blown away now when I think of that treadmill that I never stepped off for a second.

It was the Thursday before we were actually told that the funeral could go ahead. I'd thought that the coroner's report would be enough for me to obtain probate and the death certificates, but it wasn't. I was getting to the point where I didn't know what to do. I didn't know how to register their deaths to formalise everything, especially with Stu as I had to produce so much to sort things out for Elizabeth and me. I sat at my parent's dining room table, surrounded by paperwork, completely overwhelmed, when I noticed a card from my local councillor saying that if there was anything he could do to help, to give him a ring.

I did just that.

I called him and asked whether he could help. He said, 'Leave it with me.' It was one of the best calls I made. I just didn't know what to do, there was no one there to guide me but that man really did help. Every little thing just became a mission on its own but I had to get it done. I was swimming in stuff to do and I would have drowned if I had stopped. I had to try and separate the emotions so that I could just deal with things as I would with a client, I had to be pragmatic. I was the wife, I was the mother, and there were some things only I could do. With other things, people would say, 'I've contacted the florist, but what do you want?' There was only so far others could go with decisions and there was nothing that I could back out of even if I'd wanted that. I had to make the final choices for everything. In some ways that was hard but on the other hand, it was just up to me; I had no one else who might be standing in my way.

On the same day as the cyclists appeared, I had a meeting with the estate agents to see about renting a property near to my parents. I couldn't think about going home to a big, five-bedroomed house, just me and Elizabeth. I hadn't been there since it had happened and I had no plan to do so. I knew I couldn't keep staying with Mum and Dad, no matter how wonderful they were as they lived on a different time clock to me. But they found it hard that people were dropping in to see me at all hours and it was getting too much for them. I couldn't even think of returning to a house where there might still be dirty coffee cups and memories of the life we had lived until it all stopped. I couldn't go back to the place we had left with no idea that we wouldn't all be returning. At that stage, I knew I couldn't go back to that house; I couldn't think of being there, shutting that door, and being on my own with my daughter. A house that was full of love and noise and laughter would now be very, very quiet with just the two of us.

I suppose there was an element of, *If you don't go back, you don't have to deal with it*. I did need to stay in the local community though, even if some of the support was inappropriate. I felt that I had suddenly become public property and that people were vying for who knew me the best, who had known Stu the best, and who had been Fraser's best friend at school. That side of things was too much. There were also a lot of newer people who were suddenly there all the time, although they disappeared as quickly as they'd arrived once things settled down. I think they all had the best of intentions, but it was just so overwhelming.

My brother found a flat which seemed ideal as it was so nearby and close to Elizabeth's nursery. It would be a holding rental for six months to let me decide what to do with the house. It never actually happened due to the landlord, but it was a plan and it made me fall into very practical levels of coping with the future. The letting agent who was involved in the one that fell through offered to convert an annexe to his house and rent me that, but it was obviously going to take some time to sort it out. I knew I didn't want to go back to my old house but I also knew that I didn't want to have a knee-jerk reaction; renting seemed the most sensible option.

Elizabeth kept on her own track of coping; she never spoke to me about what happened that night. We did pray together every evening before bed, always doing one prayer for God to look after Daddy and Fraser, and she became quite focused on doing that every night. It was our connection together to them. She would talk about them whenever it came into her mind and she seemed older than her years at those moments. She knew that they'd gone but I didn't want to talk to her about the incident as I wanted her to know what she remembered rather than giving her my memories. I thought she'd been sleeping when it happened but how could I be sure? I'd been pushing her in a stroller in front of me, and I knew she hadn't slept all that night at the party so must have been exhausted, but I couldn't be 100% certain of what she'd seen or understood. While I was keeping a very close eye on her, I was also trying to think through every eventuality.

We had to have a meeting with the funeral director regarding all of the practicalities such as the coffins, and they were very kind and respectful. I remember saying, 'I want a white coffin for Fraser.'

'Do you want the same for Stu?' they asked.

'I do – but that makes him out to be an angel! He doesn't deserve that really, but I'll allow him it!'

It was the right thing to do. They had different colours inside, and a wreath each. Quite recently, I had a bit of a meltdown as I couldn't remember what Fraser's colours were.

I texted my sister. 'How can I have forgotten? I'm such a bad mum.'

Now I know. Stu's was the blue and white of the wickets and wheels club, in bicycle form, with his initials, whilst Fraser had FAB and red for Believe, which was also for Manchester United.

I put Fraser in his new Manchester United kit, the one that Stu's parents had bought him for Christmas. Stu was in his cycling clothes – he would have wanted to be in lycra, I knew that! I didn't bury them with anything. Fraser didn't need a bear as he *was* the bear and he had his daddy. Stu didn't need a teddy as he had our Bear. I was asked if I wanted Stu's wedding ring, which had been his great aunt Hilda's, and I did feel I needed to keep that for Elizabeth. I wanted to keep as much for her as I possibly could.

I never went to see them once they were at the funeral director. His parents and brother did the day before the funeral, but I had said goodbye to Stu when I left for Bristol with Fraser, and I'd had all that time with my boy. I also thought, as I've said, that when I identified Stu's body, he was still my Mr Wonderful. When I said goodbye to Fraser, he was still Bear. I didn't want those images to change. I wanted nothing to interfere with those memories, even if they didn't look damaged or hurt.

Stu's parents, Pat and Trevor, did visit and they told me that I wouldn't even have known that Fraser had undergone the donation operation. I now again recall the comment of 'cutting up my dead son' and find these reassurances are what is required within the organ donation world from us donor families but do wonder if I wouldn't have known? My heart would have surely told me even if my eyes had not, that he had already become my hero.

Finally, inevitably, the day came.

ANNA-LOUISE BATES

It was time to say goodbye for the last time.

Chapter Thirteen

A Funeral

The service was always going to be in St Martins, which gave us the luxury – if you can call it that – of a very big church. During that whole, horrific, utterly surreal week, I planned it all. Every choice had to be made by me, and each single one hurt.

I had to make the horrible decision of where the funeral cars would leave from. Would it be Mum and Dad's house where I'd been staying, or would it be from our home in Watkins Square? Which would be 'right'? It hit me that Stu's family had decided they would stay in my old house without me there before the funeral so they would be the occupants on that day, not Elizabeth and me. Did that mean it wasn't our home anymore, did that mean it should be the place where Stu and Fraser left for their final journey or that it shouldn't? I couldn't go back there but I hated the thought of people being around our stuff. What bed would they sleep in? What were they going to do in the house? I didn't want them there but how could I even have that conversation?

Bridget and I went shopping for a funeral dress for me at one point and her husband went to my old house to put the heating on – that was quickly how I thought of it - our 'old' house. As soon as he got there, he saw that the water tank had exploded and everywhere was flooded. I still say that was the boys! They'd decided that no one was going to stay there after all, and I didn't need to have the conversation that I dreaded.

I also had to decide which songs and music would be played and it seemed apt to go for carols and hymns with it being so close to Christmas. The date of losing them has made it a hell of a Christmas every time since when I hear those carols. I did feel that it was right to choose childlike carols that would call to both Fraser and Stu. We had 'O Little Town of Bethlehem' as the words were so pertinent.

'How silently, how silently,'
That's how the world seemed to me at that moment.
So silent. So quiet.
'The morning stars together,'
My boys. There, together, in heaven.
'The hopes and fears of all the years are met in thee tonight.'
All of my hopes and fears were certainly facing me in such stark contrast to what I'd expected my life to be, and the funeral was going to be the next stage in seeing that made flesh.

Stu's favourite carol was 'O Holy Night' and I chose that too, feeling that there was hope in those words:

'Fall on your knees, o hear the angels' voices,'

It was ironic and yet beautiful that the carol held those words 'fall on your knees' given Stu's singing of 'Fall At Your Feet' with the busker in Dublin.

Elizabeth's godmother's nephew, who was sixteen at the time, was a beautiful singer and always sang in the pantomimes with us. I rang him up and asked if he felt he could be strong enough to sing for me. 'It would be an honour,' he said. We also went for 'Silent Night' in German as that would mean a lot to Stu's parents as it was the version he sang with his dad.

We would have the fullest choir ever as people were coming back who hadn't sung for years and the church would be packed. During this meeting where I decided on the music, Steve told me that Stu's dad, Trevor, wanted to do a homily and, to be honest, I was a little knocked off by that. I was obviously preparing something for Fraser and Father Irving was preparing something independently as he knew them so well, but I hadn't accounted for Trevor speaking too.

Father Irving would read mine out on my behalf as I just felt I wouldn't be able to do it but now there was something else to consider. Everything was overwhelming with regard to what had happened and what I was now having to organise, and I wasn't sure if Pat and Trevor could appreciate the magnitude of it all. Of course, they had lost their son and grandson, I would never minimise that, but they weren't in the midst of the chaos; they weren't in the middle of a whole society that had been impacted by this and they hadn't seen just what my life had become. They were, however, adamant that Trevor would do a eulogy for Stu and I was equally adamant that my words for Fraser would be read out by Father Irving. I wanted those words to resonate rather than have people focus on my upset which is what might happen if I was the one to say them.

It was usual practice in our church to welcome the bodies of the deceased into the church the night before the funeral and it would be no different for Stu and Fraser. On the Friday night, the boys were brought in with about a hundred people waiting for them - the church family. It was going to be an important moment for me, full of peace and beauty away from all of the madness I knew could ensue the following day. It would be private because I would only be surrounded by those I thought of as family, rather like the time I'd had in the hospital.

When I arrived for the Mass, those people were already there. It was dark with lights focussing on the two coffins and the organist playing beautiful music. The service itself was quiet – a moment just to be with them. This was the time when I felt they were safe. I didn't want that service to end, just as I hadn't wanted the journey back from Bristol to end. It was a chance for me to sit in my own thoughts. When it did end, I'd have to go to bed which would mean I'd have to wake up, and when I woke up, I'd have to say a final goodbye. I just wanted to stay in that moment, to hit pause. Not knowing how the following day would go was terrifying.

That night, I wasn't on show or display. I was just allowed to be a grieving wife and mother. As I wept, I knew that the church family wasn't judging me; I could simply be.

We told the media that they could stay outside the church but would prefer if they didn't come in. You can't actually tell people that they're not allowed in a church as it's an open space that welcomes everyone, and we just hoped the journalists and photographers would accept the compromise. In my mind was also the fact that, with any funeral, there is a point when the family walks in and everyone looks at them. I didn't want that to be watched, I didn't want to feel as if I was an exhibit. But we had a plan. The vicarage backed onto the church so we decided that the funeral cars would drop everyone from the family there. We all went in by that entrance, in through my grandmother's old living quarters. Her Dutch courage was a little glass of sherry and I had one in there in memory of her, hoping that her strength would help me through.

People had started to come into the church from 7 am that morning. Tim, the organist and choirmaster, plus the choir, got there very early to sing some background songs. I didn't want us all to walk in at a certain point for the service to begin, I wanted us to just go in when we were comfortable and take our seats, then have the main group of mourners come in. I'd only been able to reserve a certain number of rows and seats and just hoped that there wouldn't be people there who had turned up for nothing more than a day out.

I don't think the media could work out what was happening. Hearses arrived but there were no coffins as the boys had been in the church since the night before. There was no funeral party, yet they could hear music from inside. They'd been completely hoodwinked and didn't get their photographs. I felt that I'd pulled off a small victory. I walked into the church and will never forget what they were singing. *'Do Not Be Afraid.'* I hadn't chosen it and in fact had never heard it before. It was the most beautiful and calming song. It was perfect.

'When the fear of loneliness is looming, Then remember I am at your side.'

I was there with my bear and two red roses which I would place on each coffin. I didn't look at the coffins but when I lifted my eyes from the flowers and looked around for the first time, I had never seen anything like it. The cloisters were full and the mourners were overflowing into the street. It was incredible but I was so proud that, in the middle of what you could almost describe as hype, I'd succeeded at managing it the way I wanted. There were no journalists or photographers in there and I could be myself.

It was the most beautiful service. Steve, Bridget, Father Irving and I can be very proud of what we created. I knew a producer who filmed the funeral, as I felt that Elizabeth shouldn't be there. She was too little, but a film could answer any questions when she was older if she wished to watch it, the opportunity would be there. I still haven't seen the video and I don't know when I'll have that strength. Maybe it will be nice one day to just watch it and have a really good cry. Maybe I never will.

I based Fraser's eulogy on what his friends had put in a memory book, and I used that to bring his personality to the fore. Father Irving's words were so relevant to the boys and I really felt that, even though it was so packed, it was personal. I felt like I was being enveloped with love and support. I felt blessed however silly that sounds. I felt there were arms all around me – Stu's, Fraser's, God's; I didn't feel alone. Not at all.

We'd had to consider whether children should be at the funeral. I knew that it wasn't appropriate for Elizabeth, there would be far too much attention and I couldn't be her one support on that day. I also felt that other children shouldn't be faced with the coffin of a child in front of them. They'd suddenly be questioning their own mortality. Through our involvement with 2Wish, I had seen how much support is needed for siblings and other young people on the death of a child, and that was something we didn't have in place. My family all seemed absolutely fine with kids not coming, as did the parents of all Fraser's school friends. Martin had arranged for the children to come to the afternoon wake at Cardiff City if they wanted. That would be the celebration and much more appropriate I felt. The club said they would take them round the stadium and changing rooms which would make it an easier day for them.

Unfortunately, not all people agreed with the stance of no children and again that really hurt but there is nothing I can do about that now.

As I've said, it was almost like planning a wedding, making sure that everyone who needed to be there was there, but – as with a wedding – there were 'sides.' Stu's parents were on the left and my family was on the right which meant that, even in our mourning and grief, we were separated.

Fraser was a seven-year-old angel. He wouldn't have been able to know what he would have wanted at his own funeral. I knew Stu had wanted cremation, but what about my little boy? That would never have entered his head. All I could do was try and reflect him, his kindness, his heart, the lives he had touched in just seven short years. He had made such a big impression for someone so young. I needed to make sure he wasn't forgotten. There was Stu, larger than life, a big-hearted Labrador who would make an impression on anyone in any room and I knew that I couldn't have him taking over the funeral. It had to be delicately done in order that they were both equally remembered and equally reflected on what they had brought to everyone's world. It made me question - at what point was I grieving for which person, for which of my boys? Most people would have had an affiliation with one or the other, but I was completely torn.

Trevor did stand up. He did read and he did do a eulogy. It's only writing this that I realised I feel like I'd never really said goodbye to Stu because of the eulogy being given by his dad but, thankfully, Father Irving's homily did speak about Stu as father and husband.

We left the church and went to the private crematorium, private to stop the media from being there. We played *500 Miles* and *Forever Young*. We had a screen showing the boys singing the songs together and some photos of them – I wanted the pictures to be of them as they were when they'd gone, not of them younger. It had to be how they were at that time, at the time they'd been taken from us all; that was incredibly important to me.

There were only a hundred people allowed at the crematorium and I had to do a guest list, again almost like preparing for a wedding. I had my family and friends alongside Fraser's headteacher and her husband to represent the school. I had to pick one school mum with another mum and her husband to represent the football club as well as someone from the Beavers and Cubs. It was a list I had to run past Pat and Trevor who had asked me to keep seats at the funeral for a coachful of fifty people, which just wasn't feasible. It wasn't a football stadium, I just didn't have space for people who had been at school with Stu over those who had actually known and loved them in recent years.

I had to choose pallbearers too for the boys at the church – Stu's ushers for him, then, for Fraser, I chose Paul who used to stay with us and had such an affection for him, my brother, my brother-in-law, and a friend of Stu. I was dreading the cremation even though it turned out to be beautiful too. Like everyone who has lost though, when the curtain comes down on your loved one, it's always the hardest.

Mum and Dad were holding me as we left with me grabbing my bear as a comfort blanket. I could cry a little more in the crem, but I never wailed. It was just a constant drip of crying, just as I'm doing as I write this. It was a constant pain, a constant ache.

It was a worry about what was coming next. I knew all about this part as I'd planned it all, but what would happen afterwards?

I was cold with dread. I'd had no time to think of whether the funeral was even going to happen, and all of the organisation, the intensity of everything, whereas now, after it had happened, I'd be in freefall.

I had done everything I could.

This was the goodbye.

I'd done them proud.

But now I had to turn and face the future without them.

Chapter Fourteen

GMTV

Elizabeth did come to the wake for a while, but it went on for ages and my parents took her back to their house. I knew that Stu would have loved it all. I played our wedding playlists with everyone's favourite songs, as well as playlists from Fraser's birth, just trying to make it a celebration of their lives.

Somehow, I got home that night, and the following day was the start of the next stage – it was a week until Christmas. At some point, Mum and Dad had put their decorations up, but I had no idea when that happened. I hated the sight of Christmas jumpers. I couldn't bear the association, but there was nothing I could do about that. There was nothing I could do about any of it. The old cliché was true – life goes on. I had to get Elizabeth's presents wrapped, I had to do her a stocking and put it out for her, and I had to face up to the fact that Fraser would never get the guitar we'd bought for him. I gave it to Steve's son, Connor, and he took it back to Ireland where the music would carry on.

When Bridget's husband Abs had gone to collect Stu's car from outside the party, he'd looked in the boot when he got home. Stu had put his presents to me in there – a pair of North Face boots and a Fitbit. Abs wrapped them up and said, 'When you're ready, they'll be there for you.' I opened them by myself on Christmas Day. My brother turned up dressed as a turkey later that day and that did make me smile. 'Stu made me do it!' he said. I think he probably did.

I've always believed that Christmas is about life and the gift of life. When I thought that there were other people that day whose lives had been changed for the better by my boys, I held onto the hope that their deaths hadn't been in vain. I don't really remember the actual day very well, but somehow, like most things at that time, I got through.

I found out around about that time that the funeral had been live-tweeted, although reporters denied it outright later on when I spoke to them.

'We would never have done that, we would never have authorised it,' I was told but it was there for everyone to see! They'd been turning to the police outside saying, 'We don't understand. There's no coffin. There's no family. What's going on?' Some outlets also denied that they had said I'd turned off Fraser's life support. All of those things happened, and they caused so much heartache. They didn't need to sensationalise it, it was horrific anyway – the facts spoke for themselves. One article was sent to me and it began, 'Anna was walking down the road. The wind was sweeping through her hair. Suddenly . . .' How could that sort of thing help anyone?

I was facing denial everywhere. When I met with people from the organ donation team and expressed how awful it had been, I was told, 'It's just how things are done – maybe you should go home and grieve?' I knew I'd have to find another way to change things in the hope that no one ever went through this again.

In January, I was invited to London to go onto *Good Morning Britain as* a friend of a friend who worked on the show and the producers got in touch through her. That was my first live interview where I couldn't predict what I was going to be asked. I did some filming the day before with my friend Jess as an introduction when we talked about Teddy's donation. It went on for hours and it was nice to be with her. They warned me there were no guarantees about it even happening as other stories could be more important, say something happened to the Queen, then I wouldn't have a slot. I took Dad with me, and the night before, in a restaurant, something hit me.

'Dad – why didn't I donate Fraser's pancreas?' It just popped into my mind. 'I donated all the other organs, but not his pancreas.'

'Don't you dare even go there,' he said. 'That you managed to donate what you did was a miracle.'

'But why not his pancreas?'

I sat there, lost in my thoughts, and trying to tug on a memory. I thought back. They had asked me, in that room, whether my seven-year-old son had done or experienced things that were just beyond imagining. They asked me the same questions that they asked about Stu. Was he a smoker? Did he have anal sex?

Through that questioning, they had dirtied things. I *know* the questions they'll ask now. The fact that I had those things thrown at me is appalling. Being angry with those questions, in turn, gave me some more anger. The queries were obviously related to whether the donor had HIV, which is why they asked whether Stu had slept with a prostitute, but it could be phrased so differently. Most people won't know if their partners cheat, will they? He'd been to Amsterdam with friends, and I know that two of the guys he went with did go to a brothel, but who would know that if they were to donate their organs?

What if your teenage child hasn't come out to you yet? I knew the process was gruelling and something had to be done, but I hadn't realised how much they had hurt me with the questions they'd raised. Now, looking back, I still think it's not appropriate to be asking those questions at all. This would turn out to be the main reason for the charity for me, the charity that was still in its infancy – something had to be done. I would have to get the government to listen to me and realise I was helping rather than just criticising. I knew in my head, the moment you complain, people switch off, but if you help, they listen to you. I had to circumnavigate, I knew that, and it was all forming in my mind from those very early days.

I had no understanding of what being on TV was going to involve; I just got told we'd be picked up in a car in the morning. I wasn't nervous as I assumed we'd get there to be fully briefed, told what questions to ask, and things. That never happened. We were whisked off to the studio and questions were fired straight at me. We were put in the Green Room and the producer told me I'd have two segments, one at 7.20 and the big one at 8.30, to try and hit different audiences. They then whisked me into hair and make-up, sat me in a chair and the lady dealing with me immediately said, 'I've been assigned to you because I'm the strong one. I did Madeleine McCann's mum when she was on.' I looked at her and her eyes filled up. I thought, *My God, you're the strong one and look how much pain you're in*. What could I do? Instantly, I knew I had to man up. If other people were upset, I couldn't wallow in it. I asked, 'Does Dad need his make-up done?'

'Is he going on?'

'Well, I did want him to hold my hand.'

'OK – let's get him done too.'

All of a sudden, we were in the studio. There was no briefing, no guide about what I'd be asked. I was just thrown into it. Bang bang bang. We had a half-time team talk before the second segment.

'Right,' Dad told me, 'We know what's going on now. What do we need to get across? What do we want our message to be?'

'The charity, we need to talk about that,' I knew. 'Bear's travels – can we discuss that?'

'Yes – we've had our first pitch, now we're going back.'

It was all very relaxed, which made me a bit clueless about being on national TV; it was easier to speak to millions without knowing it than doing the balloon release or something like that.

They asked Dad, 'Are you proud of her?' He started to talk and I wondered what he would say because he was furious about the questions I'd been asked.

'We're trying to make the pathway easier,' he replied, diplomatically.

After the second segment, Ben Shepherd stayed to talk to me which was very kind of him, and he's been very helpful from that point on. The best advice he gave me was, 'For the immediate future, only do live interviews. Nothing can be twisted if you stick to those. It's all in your own words.' I've kept that in my mind since the moment he said it.

I was then asked to speak on 5Live the following week. I know it was the 10th of January as David Bowie died, and I was pretty much the only other story on the channel for that entire day. The harsh reality was – this was the biggest thing that had ever happened to me, but it wasn't to anyone else. The world was mourning someone completely different, while my boys were all I was thinking of. All the members of the press who had been knocking on my door had now moved on; I wasn't that newsworthy anymore. They had wanted so much from me, but I know now that even when I want a little bit back, there will always be another story. My throat was hurting, my stomach wasn't great, my body was reflecting my mind, and I stayed in the Cardiff studios to do the 5Live interview. I couldn't face travelling to London.

I was a zombie at that time. There was no feeling and no emotion when I engaged with other people. I probably didn't appreciate how hard it must have been for family members like my sister, but I was so distant from everything that I couldn't have acknowledged that at the time. Everyone has a role in their family – the sensible one, the one that never reaches their full potential, the funny one, the one that kicks off at the slightest thing, and, even if you don't have that role in the other parts of your life, there is a tendency to slip back into it whenever you are with family. I had been the baby, whereas now I was carrying this tragedy and there were so many things I had to make the final decision on; it was a complete reversal of roles for my older siblings, they just couldn't do everything for me, they couldn't be the grown-ups. They had to watch me struggle with a lot. Everything, all our life roles, had to be re-evaluated.

I don't think I was feeling as much as I should have, and I don't think I quite took in that you can't change who someone is because of the situation they find themselves in. If someone has been uncaring or unkind in the past, they'll stay that way. You can't expect them to change into what you are, you can't expect them to be what you need, and, sadly, some people did fall into that category.

Did I change?

I don't know.

Whatever I did, I hauled myself over the coals thinking it wasn't right. I was crippled by the grief, and that hasn't been the same for Stu and Fraser.

When I grieve Stu, I grieve that I've lost my love; I've lost my best friend, and I've also lost Stuey, the father, the husband, and the person he was. I would get cross with some people as I felt they were grieving him from a time when they knew him, and not as the husband and father he became. That old Stu wasn't there anymore. It would be like grieving me from when I was in sixth form at school.

When I met him, he was everything. He was the kind of person who could take over the room. He craved attention and love, and I loved him for it, but he was different once I met him. By the time we got together, he had been on a course which he said was life-changing. It was called the Penny Ferguson course, and, during it, they put a group in a circle and gave them a conversational point. After ten minutes, they stopped. 'Do you realise,' one of the organisers asked Stu, 'how much you interrupt? It was twenty times in that ten-minute section. Do you realise you finished their thoughts for them on ten occasions?'

He was staggered. He had no idea, and the impact was huge. He was really affected by the phrase he was given, if you interrupt someone's thoughts, or finish their sentences, or you're too busy thinking about what you will say next rather than what they're saying now, then you have to realise this – that person had a potential flower that has withered and died.

Stu taught me that. Just by saying it, I learned something. He was a different person after that. All I saw of him and all I heard meant that, although he was still larger than life, he now had this different level of comprehension. That is one of the greatest things he taught me – the whole wither and die idea, stop trying to presume what someone else is going to say. I grieved for the man who taught me that. I grieved for the one person who would have been there supporting me. The one person I could have been supporting too. I missed that so much.

I grieved too for our development as a couple, for the many decades we would have had ahead of us. I guess the flip side was my vulnerability. If Stu hadn't passed away and Fraser had, would we have made it? Would our love story have had a sadder ending? What a thing to think. He never chose to leave me, we never chose to split up, so we can always be Romeo and Juliet. That's our ending, that movie love I was told I would never have. That fairy tale which ended so badly but did have a conclusion that, strangely, still gives that hope that relationships can be that way, hope for me that Elizabeth will find her soul mate, her everything.

Stu had an amazing 43 years on this earth. We had our challenges, but we had nothing major that we had to get over. We were never really ill, we hadn't lost anyone that close to us, our grandparents had lived to a good age and the loss of them was all natural. He'd travelled the world, he'd had so many life experiences, we'd made every day count. For Stu, he had lived – oh, he had definitely lived.

Not long after we'd lost him, I would come out with awful statements, like, 'Stu would have preferred this – he wasn't the kind of person who would sit in the corner and die of cancer.' I mean, how cruel is that? 'Stu would be loving this – he's gone out in a blaze of glory.' I said horrible things out loud to try and give myself some justification that this was better than growing old together.

With Fraser, it was so different. So, so different.

I think now, years on, the ache just gets worse, the grief gets worse. Every single year gets harder and harder. I see his school friends becoming young men, I see them deciding on their future. I try not to think this, but he really is the little boy who never grew up. Would he have been an amazing footballer, or would he be incredibly theatrical and dramatic like Elizabeth? He's never going to have his first kiss. I'll never see anything; I'll get none of it as a mum. My firstborn has gone.

After he died, it was the little things that hit me. I couldn't go to my local supermarket; I still drive to one that is further away.

With Stu, I grieved what we had, but with Fraser, I grieved what we should have had. I asked Stu all the time, 'Am I doing OK?' I missed having the other parent who is Elizabeth's blood to check with that she was coping. I needed reassurance, I needed answers, but he had gone. My Mr Wonderful had gone.

After the funeral, everyone was still very much there, and constant Believe events were happening or being organised. I'd even signed up on Boxing Day to run the World Half Marathon in March. There were distractions everywhere and I was fine with that. Mum and Dad wanted us to go to Mexico with them, but Stu and I had been there alone, and then with the kids. I decided it would be far too hard. They changed the holiday to Tenerife, a part I'd never been to before and we went in January, with my brother turning up too. Martin even got the local bar there to do a Believe event. It was everywhere whereas I was still in a trance.

But things were about to change. And then, as if I needed reminding, the driver of the car was due in court.

Chapter Fifteen

A Court Case

I didn't decide what to do with the ashes straightaway, but I thought I'd go back to the crematorium in Barry where they would be interred. It was explained to me that you only have a lease for a certain number of years and then, you can either renew it, or the plaque gets taken away. That seemed like a burden to Elizabeth after I'd gone; she'd have the decision and the costs to think of. Would she feel obligated? Would her children feel that too? It didn't seem right.

I was in a rented conversion in north Cardiff by this point and the parish priest from the church we got married in came to check on me. He said because I lived in the parish, I could have the boys buried in the local churchyard. So that's where they went, together with their headstone. I still pop there often. When we had the interment of the ashes, Father Irving did say, 'Yes, these are some of the physical ashes, but remember, they're not here.' Even so, I still thought it might be somewhere nice to go and remember them, taking Elizabeth sometimes, although that's taken years.

Looking back, I don't think I went through the recognised five stages of grief. I was stuck in denial for so long – I still am. I don't feel that I was ever angry about them being taken away and that is probably part of needing to feel things. A lot of the time, I'd think I was so blessed. We were so blessed to have that life, those years, that it felt selfish to be angry because most people never get that or experience that. I'd probably been in the lucky 1% of the world.

What we had, what we had as a family, was so utterly amazing. People might think I look back with rose-tinted glasses, but I know what we had. Everyone has those Sliding Doors moments, and I would sometimes think of those. When I closed the practices, I applied for a job with an Australian law company. They got back to me for an interview while we were on holiday, and they were in the UK. I didn't pick up the messages until we returned and by that time, they'd left for Australia again. Was that fate? If so, what part of it? Should we still be living in Australia together to this day? Or were we meant to stay here? Would it have happened there? If it had, how would I have got through without my family? So many unanswered questions.

I do believe in fate though and we'd had a few of those life-changing moments. My sister went to Aston University and so did Stu's girlfriend at the time. There were weekends when I visited, and we had worked out that we were all at the same places at the same time socialising. Years later, just a few months before we met, we'd even been in the same pub watching the rugby. Were those not the right times for us to meet? Would anything have happened? Dublin was our moment, I guess.

At this time, the charity continued snowballing but I had other decisions to make as well. I moved out from Mum and Dad's in February into a conversion and was just waiting for some time to pass. Every time I was driven anywhere near the old house, I just shuddered. Driving had always been functional rather than enjoyable for me, but since the accident, I didn't want to do it at all. I lost my confidence completely and I'd rather walk, which was odd as it all happened when we were walking.

My 40th birthday was 8th February, and I did wonder what Stu would have been planning. There would have been something, but I'll never know. A group of the school mums organised a cocktail party close to my parent's house so that I could leave whenever I wanted, which was very kind. It was robotic – actually, I think of a lot of it as robotic trauma. Everyone was saying, 'You have to celebrate your birthday because that's what they would want.' *How would you know?* I wanted to scream. I got through it but I don't think I ever hit 40. In fact, the following year, I did a '40 again' party. I feel like I've never passed that milestone birthday. For my 40th that year though, I traded in my massive car for a tiny one which helped a little, although not much.

I did wonder whether, if I changed the old house a bit, maybe I would feel more open about going back. I did a lot of alterations, but it was no good, it was still a house of memories. However, I wasn't ready to let it go just yet. Any time I had to go down there (never on my own), it was just so cold. I couldn't see it ever being warm again – how could it? How could you transition from what had happened to a normal home? Friends had cleaned everything for me after the flood. They'd taken down all the Christmas decorations, tidied it up, and made it very clinical. Maybe walking in and seeing it how we'd left it on that night would have helped; instead, everything had been swept away as if all four of us had never been there. Elizabeth started calling it the flood house, and I call it that to this day. It makes it easier to depersonalise it. It's easier to walk away from a flooded house than a happy family home.

Then, in April, while I was still struggling with house stuff, I got a call from my Family Liaison Officer's superior.

The call was cold and functional. 'I want to advise you that our investigations are complete, and we've charged the driver with death by dangerous driving as well as death by careless driving.'

I sat down, almost collapsing onto the chair. I was absolutely gobsmacked. I couldn't believe they were proceeding on such a big charge; I'd honestly thought they would drop it. I couldn't think or feel it was anybody's fault; that would have been too much to bear. If it could be someone's fault, it could have been ours. I was already thinking of what we had been through, with the media especially, and I couldn't face the thought that we'd have to go through all of that again with a trial. It would be a circus. It would be hell.

I truly didn't have the stomach for a trial. It was the last thing on earth I wanted. What would a trial do? I had no feelings of revenge at all. It was the sheer safety level of it that made me feel that way – I'd learned about the law, I knew how you would hope people were often not respectful and always challenging, but I couldn't face giving evidence. For what use? I knew in my mind and my heart that this boy hadn't left that house that night intending to kill two people when he drove. That was never his intention. If you steal, there is intent. There was no intention with this and, therefore, to me, it was more of a negligent situation – he'd been negligent, and, to me, it would be very difficult to punish someone for being negligent. That was just how I felt at the time.

I'd worked out that, if he was charged with the higher charge, that was 5-15 years in prison. If you plead guilty, your sentence is reduced. He would never plead guilty to go and serve such a long period in prison. Death by careless driving was 2-5 years. If they were going to charge him with something, I just wanted it to be one where we would all be spared a trial.

The plea hearing was on the Thursday that Stu and I were due to go on the sponsored bike ride. I knew I had to go to the hearing but there was something on the cards for afterwards. I'd been invited to a game that was happening in Runcorn between the *Hollyoaks* cast and transplant recipients – I'd been asked to go to that with Elizabeth to represent donor families. I'm a massive closet *Hollyoaks* fan and still remember when Fraser used to fall asleep to the theme tune! I decided not to take Elizabeth, but it was something that would be there for me after the plea hearing, something to deflect from it all. My brother and sister both wanted to come with their spouses to the plea hearing, but Mum and Dad didn't. I couldn't blame them.

We went into the court quite early and sat in the front row. I'd never been in a Crown Court before and Cardiff's is very impressive. I looked to the right and there was a young gentleman who looked to be about the same age as I knew the driver was. He was dressed very smartly and looked very alone. My initial feelings and thoughts were, 'Bless him, he looks so scared. I feel for him.' He didn't look at me at all.

The Family Liaison Officer came in and I whispered, 'Is that the driver over there?'

'No. He's the one that you just passed walking in here,' he said with venom. Those weren't his exact words. The phrase he used will remain between me and him.

When the driver came in – and I don't want to name him, I don't want to give him an identity in this story – he had a creased, untucked shirt, he looked dishevelled, he looked as if he couldn't care less. He certainly didn't look towards me. I felt nothing for him, nothing towards him. I had no anger. The charges were read out and, unsurprisingly, he pleaded Not Guilty to both.

I heard sobbing behind me.

It was his mother. She was sitting behind me with more members of her family; they hadn't segregated us at all. I was snotty but she was crying her heart out. The judge then said to the parties, 'I'm sure something should be considered here, something should be discussed and maybe both would like to take instructions from their representative parties.'

The next thing I remember was that we were in an office with the CPS and the barrister for the CPS. He said, 'You may not like what I'm going to suggest, but I think that the way the judge was talking, the accused should probably accept that he is guilty of careless driving but not dangerous. I think we should see if there is some manoeuvrability here.' He then explained the different levels of sentencing.

I felt like he was waiting for an argument from me, but he wasn't going to get one.

I sighed and said, 'I think that's the best way forward.'

He explained some more to me. 'You'll do a Victim Impact Statement, Anna-Louise, which will be presented to the judge upon sentencing. Someone will contact you.'

My sister-in-law said, 'Are we allowed to do one? It's affected the whole family, and someone should know that.'

Please no, I thought. Luckily, the barrister shot that down. There was no way I wanted to ask everyone how it had affected them, it would be too much. I wanted to protect them. I'm really not sure if it was agreed he would accept that lesser charge that day or another day. I think it was that day as I can only recall going to court once, but there is a jump in my mind about all of that too. Maybe it was just settled that day. I can't remember.

All I could ask the CPS barrister was, 'Will I know of any previous convictions before I write my statement?' He said I would. The Family Liaison Officer had spoken of the driver with such contempt that it had made me wonder whether he knew more. I didn't want a trial, I didn't want everything pored over, I didn't want everyone else to have to listen or see what I remembered, but I still needed to know what happened. It would take eighteen months for me to see the witness statements. I would go through over two years of never knowing what had happened.

I found out quite a while later that the well-dressed young man who I'd thought was the driver was actually a journalist who covered all the Crown Court cases and he hadn't made eye contact with me out of respect.

Another jump.

I was at the *Hollyoaks* game. It was something amazing to do after all that had gone on. Heading there on the train was pure escapism and I could almost trick myself into thinking it was all quite natural and just a fun day out. I was in a different town, surrounded by my secret idols and now meeting more people from my transplant family. I was surrounded by love from the friends that came with me. Pat and Trevor even drove over along with 'Uncle Paul', and Stu's old housemate, Gav. I was then invited into the dressing room before being given an invitation to go on set the following day. I remember they played, *Don't Stop Believing* at the start of the match and I cried a little, not only at the poignancy of the words but the fact that I used to sing that song with Stu in our kitchen. I felt I could just be me at that point, the 40-year-old who still watched 'Hollyoaks' to the dismay of her family!

I was soon brought down to earth when faced with having to write my Victim Impact Statement. I had to base it on how I was feeling rather than actual facts because I still didn't have those facts. I didn't actually know the full impact of what he had done. I only know now that it could have been avoided and that makes me so cross. No amount of time he spent in prison could ever have brought my boys back but I did feel a little bit let down that I was never really advised on what had happened. I didn't know he had a previous conviction for undertaking a bus. I told myself, like me, he would have to deal with it for the rest of his life. When we knew he was pleading guilty and it went to sentencing, the FLO came round to the house to help me with my statement.

I started with, 'I'm thankful that the driver has pleaded guilty.'

The FLO's comment will never leave me. 'Are you thankful? Do you really think the driver has pleaded guilty for you? Do you really think that's why he's done it?'

I looked at him and realised he was right. It was in my nature to hope that he was doing it to save me and to save a trial; that he was putting himself through it because I'd been through so much. My heart knew the FLO was right. We decided between us to change 'thankful' to 'relieved.' That probably was the right emotion to record anyway. We wrote the whole statement together and the sentencing trial was set for July. I'd done all I could.

'I don't want or need to be there. My statement's done.'

At the start of August, my friend Camilla suggested that ITV Wales do a documentary about everything I'd been through and the charity. 'Camilla,' I said, 'I think it's better to interview on my terms before the sentencing to get it over and done with.' She agreed and put that all in place, linking me up with the broadcaster Andrea Byrne, who became a good friend from that moment on and is now an ambassador of the charity. I knew that we had to push the positive angle of Believe. I didn't want to be defined by the court case. I wanted us to be known as the loving family we were. My brother-in-law Abs decided he would go to the court for sentencing instead.

'Will you please promise me that you won't speak to the media, even if they try to pressure you?' I asked him. 'I've made a statement that will be released by the police and that's all I need.'

'Of course, I won't,' he agreed. He had different feelings on the case. He wanted the retribution, he wanted to see him being taken down, but I didn't. I didn't want anything to undermine the memory I was trying to achieve for the boys; I didn't want everything to be focused on negativity. In the event, he only got a 24-month driving ban – it ran concurrently with his prison sentence that was sixteen months. I would have rather he had served no time but was never allowed behind the wheel of a car again.

I was never more thankful for my football than on that day. Wales had got to the semi-finals of the Euros and, on the day of sentencing, they flew into Cardiff and had a massive celebration, an open-top bus, a huge party, and front rows seats for us that evening. I was incredibly grateful not for the distraction but for the fact that our story was on page twenty-something the following day as the football took over everything. I felt like he hadn't got the airtime. That was what I needed.

The sentence was really low though; that did surprise me. Sixteen months was just so little. Matt did say to me it was at the higher level of what it could have been for careless driving, but sixteen months for two lives? All I could think was at least he wouldn't be spending Christmas with his family. He'll know what it's like to go through that without his loved ones.

In the end, he served eight months.

What upset me more was that, after those eight months, I wasn't even notified that he had been released. My sister bumped into the FLO in the local supermarket and he told her. I thought that I would have been approached before he was released on probation.

One of the reasons I was so shocked was that when I was in Spain with my sister that summer, just to make things worse, our villa was broken into. They stole everything. I had two phones at this point, one number that the media had which I needed to switch off whenever I'd had too much. They also stole my old phone. On it, I had Fraser's heartbeat that I'd recorded at the hospital, and they even stole a rucksack of Fraser's in which Elizabeth kept all her Peppa Pig toys. Fraser had written his own name in it; that was hard to lose.

When it happened, I was advised to post on local Facebook pages, asking people to look out for what had been taken. I switched on my other phone so that I could get notifications. I would happily have paid for the phone to get the photographs and heartbeat back. Stu used to do all the back-ups and I had no idea what was stored elsewhere but I was terrified I'd never get precious memories back again. I had no idea there was a notification part where people you aren't friends with can send you messages, and because I'd just put Facebook on that phone, they all came up as I was scrolling.

They went back to December.

I came to one that was from the driver's mother. She'd contacted me. She'd actually contacted me. It began, *from one mother to another*. I went white. I left my room and walked through to where everyone was playing a game of cards.

'Are you OK?' said Dad.

'No. I've been contacted by *his* mother.'

I can see where I get my often misplaced positivity from because he responded, 'Oh that was kind of her.'

At that point, I remembered exactly what Matt had said to me. 'Dad, she didn't do that for me. She did that for her.'

I immediately deleted the message and blocked her.

When I found out he had been released, I was adrift again. Wales isn't that big a place. It would have been common courtesy to inform me. I could bump into him anywhere. It was a crime against a person which I thought meant there was a duty to tell them not to contact you or come near. His mother had been in touch – would he do that too? Was I going to see him on the street? How would I deal with that?

To this day, how would I deal with that? I'd recognise him anywhere. It's etched. He's not a dementor-type figure who I fear will suck my soul from me, but I wonder how I'd react – or not react. I just have to try and live with it and hope I never will see him for the rest of my life.

By this point, things were getting too much for me. And things came to a head on Fraser's birthday – our first without him.

LIFE: A STORY OF BELIEVING

Chapter Sixteen

Pride of Britain And Joan Collins

Of course, life wasn't on hold while all of this happened with the court case. Life was still busy – and moving on.

Elizabeth's first day in school ripped my heart out. She was going to the same school that Fraser had attended, which meant that on her first day, I had to go to the same door he had gone in. I had to get my little girl ready for school and just take her when I should have been dropping off two of them. Fraser should have been starting back too.

Just dropping off one child was so hard; trying to avoid seeing any of Fraser's friends broke my heart. There wasn't a huge change in them at that age, they still looked like little boys, but they were still a reminder of how everyone else was growing up and Fraser wasn't. I had to protect myself, keeping away from the boys in the class, and the mums did shelter me. I appreciated that.

I started to wobble in the days that followed though, and I said to Dad, 'I'm stuck. I'm stuck in this rented house. I can't go home, but I know I don't want to be here. I think I need to move. Something needs to happen.' I wanted to stay in Lisvane in north Cardiff but ended up not too far away in Thornhill. As soon as I walked into that house, I felt I was home, and put an offer in on Fraser's birthday, planning to move in the week before Hallowe'en.

But making 'something happen' also meant that I'd be exposing my vulnerabilities. It was a risk, but something had to happen, or I would have been stuck there forever.

One of the school mums had invited me round for coffee and Maryland cookies (Fraser's favourites) on the day of his birthday, and then I went to the grave. Father Irving did a service and Cardiff City (where we were having the Believe Ball the following week) said we could release some Believe balloons there. I also posted balloons up to Pat and Trevor so that they could release them there too on the day. However, Fraser's birthday that year brought me my first breakdown – and it was my mum who got my wrath the night before. Everyone was trying to shield me so much, but Mum innocently slipped up and told me that my nephew would be starting Beavers on the night of his birthday. And I snapped.

'How can you do this?' I roared. 'How can you do this today of all days? How can these things be happening?'

'Yes, but life does have to move on,' Mum said.

'But mine hasn't! And I don't want it to – and it's not fair! It's not fair!' I remember being so angry and crying so hard. I've no idea how it was resolved, but I couldn't control the emotion for once. Everything hit me and, for the first time, I said it wasn't fair. I'd never said that before. Everything wasn't OK for me, it really wasn't. Maybe that was the time I could actually yell and shout and scream because I had just kept it together for so long.

At that time, I had to get the flood house ready for sale before we could move into the new one. The estate agent advised me to remove everything and sell it as an empty house, a shell – the new owners weren't going to be buying into us. I was worried we'd get grief ghouls and don't really know if that happened, but the thought of our house being described as a 'shell' hit hard. We'd had so many memories there, we'd made our wonderful life in that house, and now it was to be cleared, everything ripped away to make it a blank canvas. 'Moving on' hit me hard.

All of the initial help had gone and this was now my job, one I had to do pretty much alone. One of Stu's friends did come with his girlfriend and took lots away, but just when I thought we'd emptied the top floor, I found out that Stu had filled the loft fit to burst. Every day, I came across something - Fraser's Christening candle, all of the videos that Stu had recorded of all our family moments for years, and his wedding speech. Every little thing was a memory. But it was overwhelming.

Stu's approach to life was, 'Why have one when you can have twenty?' and my goodness, I was finding that out as I tried to clear things! He had seven guitars and four pairs of cycling sunglasses that I'd never seen that he was squirrelling away - there was just so much stuff. My garage and loft are still full of so much of it and it took until last year to get rid of Fraser's bikes. I can't face clearing out anything else. How can you throw memories away? Once I get rid of things, I can never get them back again and the fear of that is huge.

One of the things people don't understand about grieving is that there are parallel stories running at the same time – it's back again to the 'life has to move on' cliché. My grief hadn't gone anywhere, but I still had to be the best mum I could be for Elizabeth, everything was happening legally regarding the 'incident', people were coming to terms with their own loss of Stu and Fraser. There were so many things happening, and all I could do was deal with each of them as they came up. Unbeknown to me, events were taking place behind the scenes that would lead me to London - and a room full of celebrities.

At that time, I wasn't aware that one of my old Slimming World groups had a secret Facebook page called 'We All Believe in Anna-Louise Bates.' I'm so glad I didn't know about it as I would have found it too much to deal with, but it had a lot of followers and they'd decided they wanted to nominate me for *Pride of Britain* in 2016. It was the most ironic thing as it was the 2015 show that Stu had watched and that had sparked off his conversation with me about organ donation. It's where the story of Believe had started.

In October 2016, my Family Liaison Officer (FLO) asked me if I would give a talk at an event at which FLOs from all over the country listened to those who had been involved in road traffic incidents. He drove me to Birmingham and that was really hard as that was where Stu had lived when we first met. Even the drive was a struggle. Dual carriageways were bad - I'd had it in my mind that where the incident had happened was a busy dual carriageway; I figured that we must have climbed over bollards or something for the accident to happen. In my head, I'd reconciled the idea that we had been on a similar road, but I later found out that that wasn't the case. I felt like Stu was with me in Birmingham though and that was lovely.

Speaking to a roomful of police officers was challenging. Before I began my speech, I sat through them coldly relaying the facts and figures regarding road accidents. I attempted to distract myself, doodling and trying not to listen. The people speaking before me were talking about statistics and trauma, and it was all very black-and-white, such as a certain percentage of parents who lose a child in a road incident will split up. That one made me look up and take notice. Stu and I didn't choose to split up, he didn't choose to leave me, but would that have happened if he had survived? Would we have got through it? Would we have been

LIFE: A STORY OF BELIEVING

in the 12% who stay together or the 88% who don't? Maybe we wouldn't have stayed together anyway. Who knows? You can't 'what if?' everything.

I don't think I had really comprehended what I was being asked to do by Matt, and I thought that it would be another good opportunity to talk about Believe and raise awareness. It seemed such a cold environment, it was probably part of their Continual Professional Development, and I hope I provided some value, but it wasn't a warm place. A few of them asked when they should ask potential donor families about donations and all of it took me back to that night. I was in an alien environment and facing these things on my own. All I could say was that if Matt had mentioned organ donation to me immediately, that would have been awful. For me personally, I wouldn't have wanted to be asked in the Royal Glamorgan when I was told Fraser was brain dead, let alone before that – especially if it had been a police officer, not a medic. My suggestion was that if they had a Believe bear in their car, it could open up conversations. It might subliminally start the thought process in a kinder way.

Undertaking talks like the one in Birmingham, I did feel it was my purpose. I never thought of it as being *Why is this happening to me? And* I still wonder if this is all destined, if this is my purpose in life. Father Irving had told me that God would never want to cause pain, but I always ask why had I been thrown into this situation? Was it because I could do it? Sometimes, if I did falter, I would think about the bravery of Fraser and the fact that he had made it to the hospital against the odds – if he could do that, I could surely do a speech. I hate it when people say anything nice about me or what I do and I felt it throughout that day. When people say, 'I don't know how I would have dealt with the hand you've been given,' I just think, 'I hope you never have to.' But you never know what is inside of you and what you are capable of. Part of me is relieved that I've managed to do this but a much bigger part of me, naturally, hates that I've had to.

Whilst in Birmingham the four regional finalists were announced and I was doorstepped the day I got back and told that I'd won the Welsh regional category of *Pride of Britain* and was invited to the London event. The overall winner would be announced on the night. I asked my sister, Bridget, to come with me for the event the following week which was to take place on Hallowe'en. I was glad I wasn't in Cardiff for it as Hallowe'en had always been a big family event for us, even though we were Christians. In the eyes of the Church, it's an American gimmick whereas in my eyes it was a lot of fun; you can have religion and a good time, you don't have to choose. We'd all dress up and decorate the house and garden, it was such a special time for us as a family. It's also important as All Hallows' Eve, the service before All Souls' Day, when you remember the dead. In our church, there is a list where all the names of the dead are written and then read out on the day. I was relieved not to be there for that and I haven't been back for the service since the boys died.

The day of the awards arrived. Early on, we were all introduced to each other with the fifteen stories being summarised by the producer, who did it with no notes at all! These were incredible people. As soon as we heard the story of a man who had run 365 marathons in 365 days, Bridget and I looked at each other. 'It's him,' I mouthed to her – he must surely win with an achievement like that! 'Marathon Man' was still running half-marathons as he couldn't just stop immediately or his body would go into shock. He'd been bullied as a child so was raising money for an anti-bullying charity and Stonewall. Every story was unbelievable though, these were incredible human beings, and it was really humbling.

I had to deal with the sadness with black humour at times too. When we were told of a woman who had lost her entire family in a car accident, I whispered to my sister, 'Oh my goodness Bridget, I've been out-tragedied!'

I got dressed that evening in a beautiful gown – red for Believe with butterflies on it, the emblem for donor families. Taxis dropped us off around the corner and we were told to walk down a red carpet as people clapped; all of a sudden it was very real. I had a responsibility to the boys and everyone who had supported us in the past ten months. I had to make sure that I made the most of every second and get my message across to as many people as possible.

I'd taken down a little book with a picture of Stu and Fraser on the front and I planned to get some autographs if possible, but at the evening event, I decided I would be even braver and approach celebrities with my bear, hoping to get some photographs I could use for publicity. I managed to get Louis Walsh, Lesley Joseph, Mary Berry, Theresa May, Judy Murray, Ola and James Jordan, Brendan Cole, Barbara Windsor, the cast of Hollyoaks, Freddie Flintoff, Simon Cowell, and they were all so supportive. I heard many celebrities saying 'no' to people asking for photos so it wasn't a given, but I had to get our 'hook' over instantly and make them feel Believe was something they could get behind. I'd messaged Ben Shephard on the way there and asked him the best way to get pictures of our bear with celebs, and he'd got back to me saying, *You'll be absolutely fine!* and he was right. He even found us on the night and was lovely as always.

The awards started and then it hit me - I was going to have to listen to a lot of trauma. This was the show I wouldn't even watch with Stu and now I was here in person. I had always thought that if I didn't know about the stories they showcased, I could pretend bad things didn't go on in the world – and now I was here and I couldn't get away from it. I was one of those 'bad' stories. I spent more time in the toilet than in my seat, I just had to get away from it at times. *Can I deal with this one?* I asked myself before every nominee's tale was told. It was almost overwhelming. I took a breather and went to the loo again where I feared the tears would start to flow.

Joan Collins was there. I was upset but I had to ask. 'I'm sorry, but could I have a picture of you with my bear?'

She turned to me. 'Oh darling, we are in the amenities – let me just finish what I'm doing then *of course* we can have a photo!'

I was quite squiffy by that point, too nervous to eat. A couple of glasses of champagne in, and I felt like I could do this.

I took my seat.

The lights dimmed.

My heart fluttered.

It was time for the main event.

Chapter Seventeen

PTSD And A Hole In My Heart

And the winner is....

I'd been right – the winner was the 365 Marathon Man! Naturally, I was disappointed that an opportunity to get the profile of Believe raised even further had gone, but I couldn't deny that Marathon Man had done an amazing thing. It would have been a lovely achievement in memory of the boys to win, especially given the link to Stu watching the event the previous year and it being the push for him to discuss organ donation with me, but things happen for a reason.

In retrospect, I'm actually glad I didn't win; I think it would have been an even bigger place to fall from and I don't think I needed that going into the first-year anniversary; it was all a bit too quick. To be nominated and recognised now would be such an honour, but at that point, I'd just dealt with what I had to in order to get to that stage. Now, I feel I've done so much more than just survive.

The week after the Pride of Britain Awards was Guy Fawkes Night, or Guy Fawkes Week as people seem to be setting off fireworks for much longer now. The bangs were giving me terrible panic attacks. I went to the GP the following week and was finally told I had PTSD. They referred me to a counsellor for trauma therapy – I'd had nothing before that. I'd never really been checked in on at all.

I only went for a couple of sessions of therapy as there was always a medical student there. I'd agree to it because that's what I do, and then I would just be telling my story yet again. I felt I was just retelling it again for them to assess if I really had PTSD when it seemed absolutely obvious that I did.

The cynical side of me was also doubting the condition's existence at all. During my time as a solicitor, I'd honestly thought that PTSD was created by people who wanted to wring out more from their compensation claims. I decided instead to try the private route and I got my hands on the witness reports from the incident. The therapist had hoped that by me seeing them, along with doing a site visit, some of the holes in my memory could be addressed. I saw the reports the month before the second anniversary.

Matt had said to me at one point, 'You do know you're not to blame?' But no. No, I didn't know that at all. I did wonder if the driver had received therapy while I was still in limbo. He'd been sentenced in the July and, in the prison system, he'd be getting assistance to deal with something he had caused. I was going under the radar because I was 'coping' and yet my world had fallen apart. The grief and the trauma go hand in hand for me, but I guess he only had the trauma from causing the accident. I try and feel nothing about him. I need nothing from him.

In addition to this ongoing struggle, I was also facing the fact that the charity had become huge so quickly. Believe was something not only I could hold onto, but everyone could. It was a really positive legacy. I think, within a week, my brother's designers had come up with a logo. When I look at it now, it's pretty amazing. There were the two hearts inside the 'i' dot and we also had the organ donor support logo on there to make sure it wasn't lost. We got everything copyrighted and trademarked, which did take some time. At the funeral, I'd been approached by an old school friend and a lady I knew through ante-natal classes who offered to become trustees. The three of us made up the Board. All of the legalities were done quite quickly and then, a few months later, a local firm of solicitors offered me a trainee pro bono to help register the charity. That was huge as registering a charity can be a nightmare.

We were registered by June of 2016. It was all done by the time my friend Emma did her 5k which raised £35,000 for us. That was actually on Elizabeth's 4th birthday and she had the most amazing party ever. A 'Frozen' birthday cake was waiting for her and she even 'ran' half of the route with Anna and Elsa! She was surrounded by love. When we were walking around, she turned to me and said, 'Mummy, look at all these people and all this Believe. You and I did all this for Daddy and Fraser.' She could see it! I'd never seen emotional maturity in Elizabeth before the accident, but she was incredible now. A bugbear of mine was that people would say, 'Children are very resilient.' They're not. They're human beings. They just deal with things in a manner we probably all should. She could feel the love and that, to me, was so important. I don't want to say she was taking on the mantle of Fraser, but he was always so loving and giving, and she cottoned onto that.

The guy who filmed the funeral also produced one of the events, the local pub did an *It's a Knockout* day which raised a considerable amount, and everyone seemed to be contributing to this massive effort. A few months later, the Mayor contacted me and said he'd like to do an event to raise funds. It was a Night in the Mansion House, the Lord Mayor's House in Cardiff, with canapes, and music and singing. Dad, Mum, and I went for a few meetings in advance and, at the end of one meeting, someone said, 'Any other questions?'

'Yes,' Dad piped up. 'Do you have Mike Young's details? I want to contact him.'

'Mike Young, as in the guy who created SuperTed?'

'Yes, that Mike Young,' nodded Dad.

'No, I don't but I can tell you who does – the Leader of the Council.'

I looked at Dad as if he'd lost his mind; this was such a random request. Mike was Welsh and had such amazing success with SuperTed; he now lived in Los Angeles and had a production company. Dad decided to keep trying to contact him in the background while the Mayor and I looked into what else needed to be done.

After my appearance on GMB, a woman called Carrie who worked at the BBC approached me as she was working on a series called 'The Greatest Gift'; our story was going to be integrated within that. I met lots of people through it, and what became clear from the other side was that everyone was really happy that Wales had become opt-out, but there was nothing in our education system that would help people to discuss the issue, and to help children to be informed. This seemed, to me, a way I could assist very easily in trying to raise awareness without talking about the negativity and difficulties I'd had with the donation process.

I could see that education was the key angle to take. I started to meet up with different people and realised that this was the way forward. The Mayor told me that he had arranged a meeting with the Leader, the Deputy Leader of the Council, the Director of Education, and he wanted me to do a presentation for them. I went to another friend from church, Alan, who was an ex-deputy headteacher. He knew the curriculum was about to change and it was a perfect opportunity. We worked really hard on the presentation and emphasised that we weren't just talking about organ donation - we were making better citizens through encouraging debate and awareness, teaching them about informed choices and their own options in life regarding taboo subjects.

I was really nervous when I went in, but the presentation was pretty much like pushing an open door. Everybody was just flabbergasted that we had nothing in Wales. They were shocked by the misconceptions around the opt-out programme and desperately wanted to help. A lot of people – medics, nursing students, police officers – simply didn't understand what opt-out meant. They often thought that meant the conversation wasn't needed, that the next of kin wouldn't be approached, and that things would just automatically be done. That remains the confusion and it isn't the case. Next of kin can just say 'no', they don't have to justify it. When I said 'yes' at the point of identifying Stu's body, I thought everything would go ahead. Some of what could have been utilised wasn't, even though I consented. It's not a conversation you want to have for the first time when you're at hospital. It needs to be developed from as early an age as possible. Children will talk about things which scare adults, or that they shy away from, and I wanted to access that openness.

I was asked to speak at the National Headteachers Conference in April 2017 as well as many other things, and I said 'yes' to it all. The boys were there supporting me and pushing me on, and I never thought I couldn't do this. I went up to every celebrity I met, I got everyone to have a selfie taken with Fraser Bear - I was on a mission.

There was a Facebook Fraser page by then to see how far he was travelling around the world, and we also had our own Believe bears with their little red jumpers. I also had one with a white jumper, just for me, which Bear Grylls signed. He'd been so supportive throughout and even sent me a letter before the funeral, thanking Fraser for his help with the Scouting movement. I had the idea that I'd really like to work on a bear badge for the Scouting movement to do with organ donation and he's the Scouting Lead – I put that away as something for the future.

All of this was going on, it was frantic, and it was becoming huge – but there, in the middle, was the hole in my heart that wasn't healing. People could see me 'cope', they could see me achieving things. I did talks and presentations, I came up with wonderful ideas and went to events. But I was lost.

Grief doesn't go away in a linear fashion. You don't take a step forward, one after the other. There were days when I would do so much, then walk in the door at home and it was as if grief was sitting on a chair waiting for me. My old friend would hit me in the chest, knock the legs from me, wind me, and make me realise that this was going nowhere. I couldn't be 'fixed' by an award or an achievement, my boys had gone, and I sometimes felt as if I was the only one who remembered that.

And then, life took another unexpected turn when we had a message from the other side of the Atlantic.

Chapter Eighteen

Games And A Search For A Voice

In April, I'd been to a football match that saw organ recipients and donors playing against celebrities. It was the first time I'd had anything to do with the transplant sports world. I found it a nice distraction and I started to get a lot of support from people involved with it all. I made friends I could talk to who understood to some extent, and even met a man who had received a heart twenty years ago, which gave me cause for reflection.

I thought about the recipients of Fraser's organs and how long they would be given an extra chance at life because of his gifts. When I was grieving, I was grieving. When I was thinking about the boys, I was thinking about the boys. I wasn't thinking of those who had received organs all the time, but when you're in those situations, suddenly it's like a wet kipper in the face. *Wow, one of these people could actually be here because of Fraser*, I thought as I watched the games. That was a real possibility because it's all anonymous, you don't know where the organs have gone.

A lot of them did struggle talking to me because I'd lost a child. I could immediately understand a little more about survivor guilt as I could see it in their eyes. The more people I met, the more common I realised it was for people to correspond with the family of the recipient. Many people were telling me that they had received the greatest gift of all, and many of them said there was no reason someone shouldn't write to a family and say that. It did all make me think about those letters that were mentioned – how could you even start them? I did wonder if I would get one someday, even if I didn't wonder exactly about how the lives of the recipients were. The ball was in their court, the gift had been given, and that was easier than me having to do something with it. For once, there was nothing for me to organise.

I desperately wanted a letter though and that was a stance that changed within me once I got integrated into the transplant world. There is a process that has to be followed. Recipients send a letter to the central body, often with the help of a donation nurse, to make sure there are no personal facts in there. They also can't say where the organ has come from.

To begin with, I wasn't as invested, but that was changing.

The following September, I was at an event in Glasgow, the Transplant Games, and heard much more from people who wrote to donor families. All of the competitors walk in, like the Olympic

Games, children and adults, and the last people are the actual donor families. It's such a grounding and emotional experience. Everyone just stands and claps and you're given the utmost respect. I was part of all that, I walked in with them and was completely overwhelmed. With thousands of people at the games in Glasgow, it hit me again – one of Fraser's recipients could be in this room.

I'd had no communication with my own organ donation nurse by that point but I did have good communication with the Welsh organ donation nurses through the charity work I was doing. I asked if anyone had written to me as I was worried that maybe, because there always seemed to be admin issues; maybe someone had written and it hadn't got to me? Some of the people I now knew said that they had indeed written but got no reply. I knew that I'd feel awful if someone had gone through all of that, all of the struggle to write, and I hadn't replied. My friend Kimberley who had a double lung transplant, had written quite often but never had a response although that never stopped her writing and never will, but I didn't want any other family to feel they were being ignored by me.

I contacted the Welsh organ donation nurses who actually telephoned me a week before Fraser's 9th birthday to advise me that sadly Fraser's lung recipient had passed away, but that all the other donations were successful. Being telephoned with this information without notice and preparation still upsets me. And I still didn't have any direct contact.

After Covid, I requested more of an update, especially as I had not received any update on Stuey's donation. The response I got was this:

Dear Anna –

This letter contains information about those people who have benefitted following Fraser's donation.

The boy who received a heart transplant is in good health and was last seen for his annual follow-up appointment in December.

The lady who received a kidney transplant is said to be doing extremely well.

The young girl who received a kidney and liver transplant is said to be in good health and attended her latest follow-up appointment earlier this month.

I am pleased to tell you that Fraser's eye tissue was able to be used, although we have no further information regarding the recipient, we will endeavour to contact you should this become available in the future.

I am sorry to tell you that sadly, the young gentleman who received a dual lung transplant has since passed away and, unfortunately, upon clinical inspection, Stuey's heart tissue was deemed unsuitable for transplantation and was therefore respectfully disposed of.

Although I am aware that the news I have shared with you is mixed, I hope that you can take some comfort in the knowledge that Fraser's generous gifts have helped others and that the recipient of his lungs had the chance to lead a normal life and spend extra time with his family he would not have otherwise had.

    I found that quite cold. The right words were there but something was lacking. It was very basic. I didn't really know how to deal with it. I wasn't upset strangely, I just tried to deal with how I wanted to deal with it, if that makes sense. I still don't know how to process it but I don't have to, I can just let it sit there.

    I should have been furious that they hadn't told me that they had disposed of Stu's tissue, that they had taken so long to inform me, but I wasn't. I just pushed it to one side. I went through two hours of hell in that hospital for them to write so coldly – why was I not getting cross about it?

    Maybe I knew that I couldn't do anything with anger. I couldn't express it because if I ranted about it, it could affect people wanting to donate. It could take away positive memories of what I'd managed to achieve but I also knew I had to tiptoe around things all the time. I was in the midst of creating a magical transplant world charity that would only grow, and I had seen the good already. I had seen it change lives, but the price for me was that I couldn't get angry when things hurt. I knew they were under-resourced, but there were things that could be changed, and no one should be told such news in the way that I was; there should be more compassion. It was a huge blow.

    I could see things from their perspective. They were trying to do the right thing I suppose, giving me positive news about the others, but for me, that was difficult to read. I managed to convince myself that the little boy who had died did at least get 18 months he wouldn't have had if Fraser hadn't given his organs.

My mind was distracted from all of this when finally, contact was made with Mike Young and we could follow through on Dad's idea of marrying up Fraser Bear and SuperTed. Mike asked if we could Skype and I obviously agreed. I told him everything that had happened and was delighted when he said he would help out, although what came next was another thing that I was just thrown into.

'I want to do a public service announcement,' said Mike. 'I did one with SuperTed about road safety – I want to do something like that for you. Go write me a script. One or two minutes will do, get the message across, and get back to me.'

I put the phone down and wondered what in the world I'd got into this time. As soon as I started thinking about it, I knew it would have to be in Fraser's voice, from his perspective. It would be absolutely ideal to do it with words and things that Fraser would say. He would obviously talk about his heart, his lungs, his love of football and singing and dancing, connecting in all the elements of him.

I sent what I'd come up with to Mike but didn't hear anything until a few months later when I had an email back with the script 'blocked' as if it was all sorted for filming. We had another call and discussed the animation. 'It's time for you to get someone to voice the bear – you'll have to find an actor,' Mike told me.

'I don't think that would be right – it needs to be a child and it needs to be natural,' I replied. 'The voice has to sound absolutely perfect.' I then had another flash of intuition. 'It needs to be a child who isn't involved in any casting agency. It needs to be someone local.'

I had been thrown in at the deep end from the start – write a script and now find an actor! I had to take it all in my stride as it was the right stage for the charity and something positive to do. I talked to Stu and Fraser about it all the time. I just wanted to make sure it was perfect – for them. I was told by the Government that it needed to be in Welsh as well as English, which meant that I'd have to find someone with a Welsh accent who could pronounce everything appropriately.

I got in touch with the Director of Education and explained the project to him. 'I'd like to find someone who has Welsh roots, someone who can really bring this alive.'

'We'll do anything we can to help you,' I was told. I was given access to five High Schools to meet their Year 7s. I don't suppose I was making anything easy for myself, but Stu always did say, 'Push the envelope.' If it was going to be right, I was sure this was the way to go about it. I had to go into each school twice, the first visit being to tell the schoolkids what was happening and to ask whether they'd like to audition the next time I was there. That meant that I had to relive the story every time, giving them all the background so that they had an understanding of what the animation was about.

The process was amazing as the children were all telling me such incredible stories. One girl had just lost her baby brother and wanted to do something positive for him; so many of them had lost someone. Every single one of those kids touched me and they really got what I was trying to do. I'd thought that the voice needed to sound like Fraser but once I heard the kids, I realised that wasn't the case – they just needed to be able to reflect the love, the heart, the feelings of the project. I opened my mind at that point and in the last school we went to (actually my old school where Fraser would have gone), Dylan walked in.

He said to me straight away, 'My cousin was friends with Fraser and I know how much love he had for Fraser. I wanted to do something for him.' I knew from the moment I heard him that it was Dylan, he was perfect. We did a sort of 'X Factor' final audition session at Cardiff City Football Club, and all of the judges agreed with me. He was the one.

But I still questioned every decision I made. I was doubting myself. 'I've got a once-in-a-lifetime chance of documenting this,' I told myself. 'How do I do that best?' It was getting bigger all the time and, I'll be honest, I was scared of losing control over something that mattered so much to me. Mike's team did understand my vision – but they needed a storyboard. That was my next challenge! I decided it would be great to integrate Fraser's story with that of other families who had received organs and to film a documentary that could run alongside the development of the animation. This could then be used as an educational tool as well as the animation itself.

It all kept me incredibly busy, but I wondered whether it was stopping me from looking at the emotional side of everything. Where was my grief at that stage? Was I avoiding it?

I soon discovered that it wasn't avoiding me.

A short while later, I would find out that Fraser's donated heart was still beating.

Chapter Nineteen

Letters

I still hadn't received any letters about the boys' donations which bewildered me and was very hurtful. How could there be radio silence when they had given so much when they had given everything? After attending the Transplant Games in Glasgow in 2017, I enquired with the Welsh NHSBT as to whether anyone had written to me – I was worried that something could have got lost in the system.

Finally, I received a call – I was told, very coldly, that the recipient of Fraser's lung donation had died. To add insult to injury, this was relayed to me just a few days before what would have been my little boy's 9th birthday.

Finally, a Specialist Nurse wrote to me:

Dear Anna –

I hope that you and your family are well. I am writing to you today as we have received a letter from the recipient who received a heart transplant following your son, Fraser's donation.

You will find the letter in a separate envelope so that you can open this and read it at a time that is right for you.

Should you wish to reply, I have enclosed the leaflet information for families who wish to write to transplant recipients. You do not have to reply, however, the leaflet has been designed to give you some guidance should you wish to do so. I hope that this provides you with all the information that you need, however, if you require any assistance composing your reply then please do not hesitate to contact me.

The letter to me read:

Dear Donor Family –

I'm so sorry this letter has taken nearly a year to arrive. It's not that we didn't want to write, I just couldn't find the strength and words to write. How do you thank someone who gave your child a chance at life?

'Thank you' – these two words seem so inadequate for the gift of life you have given to us. You have given us a second chance to live with many happy tomorrows. We as a family will be able to see the sun rise and set, allow him to feel the rain and sun on his face, hear the wind in the trees, and listen to the birds sing. He will be able to hug and be hugged.

We must offer our deepest sympathy for your loss, mere words from strangers, but heartfelt just the same. Perhaps with your generous donation, your family and mine will be able to 'Celebrate the Life' of loved ones both past and present.

We would love to learn about the donor, we already know that they have been kind, caring, compassionate and generous, something they had to have learned from you, their family. We feel that each new day has endless possibilities and that his strength to thrive gives us the strength to learn and deal with everything he is throwing at us. I only hope that we are able to justify the use of this wonderful gift.

We all know that time can cause us to forget, but know this - not a day nor an hour or a minute will go by or has gone by without all or one of us thinking of the donor and their family who without we would not have had a chance to live as a family at home.

The above letter is everything a Google 'template of a donor-recipient letter' expects me to say and I suppose follows guidelines to the letter. Following these rules, you don't get a real sense of our feelings.

Your family's decision to do this gave me every milestone, every smile, every cry, every bump and fall all while learning. I get to feel and in our case, see this bouncy healthy special heart that although the first owner was too great to stay on this earth, they left the most valuable thing to not one but now two families. Every day I hold my baby against me I can feel this special thud, thud, thud every minute of joy I get from this reminds me of first your sadness, then a rush of the strength you must have found in a very dark place. I hope this strength is passed on through the love of the first chapters of this heart's life.

We as a family would like to learn and teach our boys the background of where this special heart came from and would be honoured to stay in touch. We honestly can't thank you more for finding the light in your darkest hour and giving our boys a chance to thrive together.

Thank you from the bottom of our hearts.

The recipient's family

In the envelope was also the information leaflet for me, should I choose to reply, which read:

The NHS provide a document for families who wish to write to the transplant recipients.

This leaflet is designed to provide you with some guidance should you wish to write to any of the people who received transplants as a result of your relative/loved one's donations.

There is no obligation to respond. This is a personal choice that you can make at any time. The Specialist Nurse involved in your care will be able to help you in compiling a letter if you want them to.

The following guidelines are to protect the anonymity of both you and the recipient(s), therefore identifiable information should not be included within the letter.

Please provide general information only, which may include:

- *The first name of your relative/loved one who donated*
- *The relationship with your relative/loved one*
- *Their interests/hobbies*

- Something about your family eg. children, grandchildren (please do not include last names)

When closing your letter:
- Sign your first name only
- Do not put your address, city, phone number, e-mail address, or the name of the hospital, or the date that your relative/loved one died

Then:

Place your letter in an unsealed envelope and on a separate piece of paper please write:
- Your full name
- The full name of your relative/loved one
- The date of donation

Place this sheet and your letter to the recipient in an envelope and send to the Specialist Nurse at the Donor Records Department.

Please bear in mind:
- The letter you send will be read by a Specialist Nurse. This is why you have been asked to send it in an unsealed envelope.
- Upon receipt of the letter, the Specialist Nurse will forward your letter to the hospital or healthcare team caring for the recipient(s).
- In some circumstances, the recipient(s) may not wish to receive your letter. This can be for a variety of personal reasons. In these cases, your letter will be retained by the team caring for them in case they wish to see it in the future. Should the recipient(s) wish to

receive the letter, the team caring for them will forward your letter onto them.

- You may or may not get a response from the recipient(s). As explained above, sometimes recipients feel very overwhelmed by the transplant process. If recipients respond, it may take months, or even years before they do. Should you wish to contact the Specialist Nurse for any further help or guidance, please do not hesitate to do so.

It was two years after the donation, two years which had seemed like a lifetime. The letter however did help me as I'd been on holiday over the anniversary, dreading the date. I wrote back to the family on 20th December 2017.

Dear recipient family

Thank you so much for taking the time and sending your letter to us at such a difficult time for us all.

Following Fraser's donation, I have met with other transplant recipients and can only imagine how hard it must be to put in writing how you are feeling but I must say that your words really did bring me so much comfort.

Fraser (my son) really did have the biggest heart. He was older than his seven years, had the sensitivity of a boy that was unmatched and was best friend to everyone whatever their ages.

He appreciated what a gift life was and really valued this gift. We, as a family, treasured and loved every minute and I am truly blessed to have had him as my son.

My late husband and I nicknamed him Bear after the House of Fraser 'bear' and love of Bear Grylls. How fitting then for bear to have become a very keen outdoor beaver, loving every minute of scouting and every new adventure.

When he and his dad passed away, his classmates wrote me cards about how they remembered Fraser. Loud, full of life, and caring were the ones that really came through. Fraser looked after the children with hearing problems, those being bullied and was very, very proud of his little sister, Elizabeth.

Fraser showed such unbelievable strength to allow me to donate his organs and I know he is looking down with pride knowing that I was able to fulfil his wishes.

Knowing that the loss of my boys has allowed yours to thrive makes me even more proud of my superstar Fraser.

I would love to keep in touch and very much hope that this letter finds you before Christmas, because this Christmas as those before, Elizabeth and I continue to celebrate the gift of life.

Anna-Louise x

Now, I just had to wait.

Chapter Twenty

Snow And A Message

Mike wanted to market the animation – and the message of it – globally, and we decided that Castell Coch would be the perfect place, a red, fairytale castle, like something out of a Disney film, to be the main setting.

Just two weeks before the launch in March 2018, Elizabeth and I went out to stay with Mike in Los Angeles to go over things. Again, this was just another thing on my list on 'new normal', things which were actually very much not normal at all for someone like me. I'd been thrown into it; I was still this little girl from Cardiff and I was only doing it for my boys, just like everything I'd done from the start.

The first time I saw the full animation with the voice and all of the parts that made it incredibly special, it hit me like a brick wall. I was in Mike's office watching it on a huge screen when the tears started to fall. I'm blown away by it all to this day and I can feel the emotion of that viewing even now. I felt at ease with Mike and his team, they were amazingly kind and supportive, and I didn't have to hide anything. I didn't have to be strong. I was able to let it all out – I couldn't have stopped it anyway. It was like a tidal wave of every emotion I could have experienced. I knew Fraser was with me, I just knew it. To see the picture of the boys at the end was an added stab to the heart as that picture always got me. However, it made me feel they were there, that they were part of this.

Mike never charged a penny for any of it. He had (and still has) a heart of gold and could see straightaway that this would help people have conversations about donating their organs; it was important to him too.

After we'd watched the animation a few times, Elizabeth and I went to a beautiful park in Calabasas, just to spend some time alone together in the middle of all the madness. She turned to me and said, 'Mum, was the reason Daddy and Fraser died was because you took me out of the car first?'

The question came from nowhere.

I'd never asked or assumed what she knew about that fateful night, but something in our trip and watching the animation had obviously led my little girl to raise something that had been playing on her mind.

'Did Daddy and Fraser not get out of the car and that's why they died?'

'Do you not remember what happened?' I asked her.

We had our own vital conversation that sunny day and Elizabeth confirmed to me that she didn't understand what had happened. She'd thought we'd all been in a car together. She had a lot of questions – which actually then led onto the topic of organ donation. She wanted to know where Fraser was now that his heart was in another child. I'll always remember that day of being around that lake, talking to her in that beautiful environment and letting it all come organically from her. It was a perfect mother and daughter time. Our bond got even stronger that day and I felt such relief that she couldn't remember.

During the conversation, I never said they were lost, as that meant they could be found again. I told her that they're very much around us, but they're not here. Stu always told me to show your faith by the way you live, and that's what I try to carry on with Elizabeth.

Be kind.

Life is a gift.

Now, it was time for the next step.

It was time for the boys to go out into the world.

I had no idea how amazing the animation would be. After all Mike's hard work, I wanted to make sure it was launched with bells on. We decided that Cardiff Castle would be the best place as there were such special memories there for me. It was where my wedding reception with Stu had taken place, and we duly invited lots of dignitaries as well as everyone connected to the charity for the launch. Mike flew over from Los Angeles and it was all systems go.

We'd organised for the animated bear to be beamed onto the keep inside the castle and then shown on a rolling basis inside the Visitor's Centre in the castle for everyone to see all night. For me, it was almost like the preparation for the crematorium as I had to make sure everyone that should be there was there; I was balancing multiple plates at once, as usual. I did send the animation to close family members so that they weren't being hit by it for the first time on the night.

I dropped everything off the day before and steeled myself for what was coming – but unfortunately, the rest of Cardiff was bracing for something else. The weather forecasts for the next day, launch day, seemed to dominate every news bulletin. I'd never heard anything like it and everyone seemed to constantly say, 'There's a snowstorm coming.'

'We've had snow before!' I dismissively said to them all. 'We'll cope. It's March, I can't remember it snowing badly for decades at this time of the year. Nothing will stop this launch.'

Mike picked me up in the morning to do some press interviews together, and we both agreed that a little bit of dodgy weather wasn't going to prevent us from making this a huge success. Everything was set – even ITV were going to be there to do a live launch. As we started to drive from one interview to another, the sky seemed to get fuller and fuller, and then the snow began. My phone was ringing constantly, with trustees starting to worry and the PA from Cardiff Castle asking what I wanted to do. Stu's parents said they wouldn't travel due to the weather and others said that they'd been advised against it too. I couldn't give up. It was *just snow*. It was up to me to make the call and say it wasn't happening, but I just couldn't do it. I decided to leave it in the hands of the Castle and see what they said.

The call came in that afternoon. They weren't able to open to the public. There was simply nothing I could do about the event but I still needed to launch the animation - that couldn't be stopped. Every button was pressed that night in my kitchen by a friend and that was it. It was just me and a few friends - even my parents couldn't come because of the snow.

I was gutted. I can't deny it was a huge anti-climax. I never got the big finale of the animation that I had hoped for – upsetting is such an understatement. It didn't even get any press attention as the weather was front and centre of everything and it would be about four days before there was any coverage. I felt so let down by it just not being enough of a story to override some snow. All of my hard work didn't seem to deserve five minutes and it really set me back emotionally. Did none of it mean anything? That conflicted so much with watching it in my own home and seeing the shares and views go up by the second, the comments rolling in, the message getting out.

Then, later that night, I had a message from Laura, the PA.

We've had a private message on the Fraser Bear social media page. I wanted to send it to you in case you miss it with everything else that is going on this evening.

And that was a message that would change everything – yet again.

It was from the mum of the little boy who had received Fraser's heart, who had sent me the anonymous letter through the organ donation team, but who was now making direct contact. She was called Zoe and her little boy was Roman. Just knowing that was incredible, just knowing who now had Fraser's heart. Zoe had only been told that the heart had come from another boy but as there are very few children's hearts out there, once she saw the media coverage about what had happened to our family, she put two and two together quite easily.

I could now contact Zoe if I wanted, we could liaise through the Believe page – but I wasn't there at that point; I wasn't at the stage where I could do that. I was blown away by the fact that I could now find out anything about Fraser's recipient so I went and looked on her social media straight away. I just needed to. When I saw pictures of Roman as I was scrolling through, I just felt sheer happiness at first. I didn't allow myself to feel too much as I was so scared as my emotions were all over the place – but I quickly also saw that he wasn't well. Roman had been given Fraser's heart when he was only a baby, and many health problems had developed since.

I was faced with a whirlwind of thoughts, particularly the one that instantly filled my head when I saw pictures of Roman, that he was a very ill little boy, and his survival wasn't guaranteed at all.

I was, once again, dealing with many, many things at once. I had built myself up so much, adrenalin-wise, to the launch. I used to always think that once something was done, I would allow myself to have that closure and allow myself to move on to the next chapter. Everyone tells you that will be the process – you start to think, once I do this thing, I can move on to whatever is next. I can look at where my life, my direction, and where I should be going with Elizabeth. But the animation didn't give me closure as it had been so different from what I expected.

I didn't have the happy ending I planned for the documentary, for the storyboard, which should also be released. I felt like I was in purgatory; I felt like I could never get that step up to heaven. I was still there. Still treading water, still trying to deal with my emotions as I was still in it. I still couldn't accept it all. It was all so personal just to me and that made it really hard to open up and talk. And now this – now Roman and Zoe.

My protective wall was being built even faster at that point; I couldn't even see the top. I felt really angry at the weather, so angry. It was something I couldn't control – again. That has a cumulative effect when something else that can't be controlled has such an impact. I had to re-finalise the documentary I'd planned which actually never went anywhere, not yet at least. We never got the right platform. We launched at the Senedd and had the backing of the AM, but nobody really gave a shit to be quite honest. All of that hard work seemed to be for nothing. I struggled quite a lot with that.

When a tragedy happens, you're showered with emotions and constant harassment from the media, things such as the live tweeting of the funeral, but when I had something positive, something that could make such a difference to people's worlds, no one cared. It makes you feel so lonely, you've been pushed up there by people being around all the time as well as the media, then, all of a sudden when you have a really positive thing to share – nothing. We were last year's news. I didn't feel I was letting the boys down but I felt let down by society and, from that point, I did start looking at a lot of things quite negatively.

During that time, Zoe and I began sending occasional messages to each other. We had a lot of shared liked pages, such as donation pages, but I didn't particularly want to give up this final bit of privacy by letting everyone else know that we were in touch with each other. We knew who we were but no one else did. It gave me a bit of control back, this was something I could determine, something nobody could take away from me; this was mine, only mine. It wasn't about taking on board or accounting for, anyone else's feelings and it was kind of empowering to have that.

It went back and forth with general messaging between me and Zoe for a while and then, during the summer after the animation,

I got a call from a reporter at *The Daily Mail* who said they were running an article on organ donation and they were featuring Roman's case alongside others. Zoe had given them my name and said that Roman's heart had come from Fraser. I wasn't happy with that, to be honest or that the reporter wanted to name Fraser in the article.

To be fair, when I said 'No', they didn't, and they didn't have to stick with that really, so I have to give them that acknowledgement. I didn't want a little mention of Fraser thrown in there. He deserved more, I didn't want him to be lost again. I wanted to protect Roman too; I'd had so much media intrusion at the beginning that I didn't know how safe he would be in the eye of that. If, all of a sudden, Zoe's family was going to be bombarded by the press and media who would know he had Fraser's heart, Roman would be defenceless. I felt I didn't know Zoe enough to advise her so I had to do what I thought was right.

From what I could see on social media, she seemed young as well as having a young family and I just felt she would be thrown to the lions. Thankfully, the newspaper article just said that Roman had received his heart from another child. I was so grateful they'd kept it that way and said, that if I ever wanted to talk about it, I'd speak to them first.

That settled that but things were changing, life was moving on. Something big was coming my way again and there was nothing I could do to stop it.

Chapter Twenty-One

Zach

With support groups, I always had that feeling that people were competing – my husband was better, my wife did more, our grief is bigger; it was really similar to school gate mums or nursery mums who would compete that their child was reading 'War and Peace' when they were four, or out of nappies when they were a month old. These groups weren't for me, but I felt that I needed something to stop me from feeling incredibly empty and I probably kept going to them for longer than I should.

About a year after the boys had passed, I was – naturally - still incredibly lonely and started dating someone for nothing more than companionship. I don't mean this horribly, but he was no Stu. It was clear he was never going to measure up. In fact, he was quite hurtful to me. I once came out of a therapy session and said to him, 'It's suddenly struck me that I won't be anyone's priority ever again.'

'Well, you'll never be mine,' he replied.

At the time, I couldn't see how wrong he was for me, I just needed someone there occasionally who would break the loneliness just a little. I felt desperately empty. He decided to end it not long after the animation, and I felt utterly lost, abandoned, and alone. Even though he wasn't right for me, he was *a* person. I still went out with friends and even went speed-dating one night. Every single man I spoke to I knew or they said, 'I know you, I know who you are.' It was a constant litany of, 'I'm so sorry for your loss.' It was a nightmare. Who on earth would date me with all of those preconceptions of who I was, either that I was brave and tough or strong, or too much still in love with Stu, or using me in a horrible way to highlight their own 'credentials' in the local community, as had already been done by other people? I was stuck. I was lonely and I was stuck. At weekends, when everyone got on with their normal lives, I felt a hole inside of me that just couldn't be filled.

I reckon I was contacted by every ex-military American in the world. Conmen were constantly in my inbox, and although I could laugh, it didn't take away from what I was genuinely feeling. I had to protect Elizabeth too - I couldn't just go into a relationship, but I wanted someone I could talk to at eleven o'clock at night. I also didn't know how to date. I'd known my first husband for years before we got together, and I'd met Stu outside a pub on a weekend away. I didn't understand the world of people getting together, where online dating sites meant you'd be bombarded with disgusting pictures and requests from strangers within seconds. This was another world to me that had evolved without me having any idea.

I wasn't made for places like Tinder. A friend came round one evening and said there was a new app which gave more control to women – you had to swipe them first and they couldn't just send messages out of nowhere. Friends encouraged me to sign up, and they said they would deal with it all for me. It was just a bit of fun but I couldn't be me. I signed up as 'Emma' who lived in a different area, and there was nothing that could link me back to who I was. A friend swiped a few of them for me and screened the messages, but even that didn't screen them all out. One guy asked what I was looking for and I said, 'Some intellectual stimulation' and even that sent him straight into sending me nasty pictures.

Then, after a friend had swiped for me on one message, a guy called Zach started talking to me.

When he asked what I was looking for, I gave him my usual screening response of *Intellectual stimulation*.

'I don't know if you'll get that from me,' he replied. 'I'm ex-RAF!'

We started but the questions that always rocked me were the inevitable ones.

Are you single?

Do you have kids?

There is always that. And I always answer honestly. It doesn't matter how uncomfortable someone gets. If you ask how many children I have, or if Elizabeth is my only one, I'll be truthful. 'She has an older brother but he passed away.' I will never act as if Fraser never existed. Zach had asked the question now. The wall had to come down and he'd have to know I wasn't Emma.

It's complicated, I wrote. *Maybe we need to have a call?*

Zach called me and it lasted for four hours. He listened to me, and he also revealed something else which would fundamentally change everything between us. Zach had cancer.

He'd contracted it whilst working in the RAF, through the fumes in the helicopters. He didn't tell me much about his cancer, just that it had 'settled.' He had a wonderful understanding tone of voice, he joked and said it was his radio voice that he used for the helicopters.

We met in the November, went for a walk together, and Zach asked whether he could take a bear onto the Coastguard Search and Rescue helicopters with him. We started to message each other even more. It was refreshing, it was lovely – but I didn't fall for him. I thought he was nice, I thought he was friendly and kind from the start, but I wasn't one to fall madly in love from the start anyway. People so often don't have the right responses, they don't say the right things when I tell them about Stu and Fraser, but Zach just asked what he could do to help. He didn't push into my feelings, he just accepted what had happened. I think I also felt at ease talking to him as I knew he was used to dealing with trauma through his work. In fact, he joked that he had a long list of 'red line entries' meaning all the operational flights, rescue, and combat missions he'd been on. Zach had even been involved in the winklepickers tragedy where immigrants had drowned, and at the Virgin train crash. Although he hadn't been in a military zone, he was used to trauma and had his own with his cancer.

We talked constantly. I finally had someone to connect with in those dark times and he was also really interesting. I didn't have to talk about myself all the time to keep things going, he had so many stories about things he'd done. He didn't know anything about me and he didn't want to. I said to him at one point, 'I bet you've Googled me.'

'Why would I do that? I want to get to know you – why would I want to do that any other way?'

I just felt I had someone there. Zach started to confide in me about his acrimonious divorce and the child custody dispute that was going on. He also had an ongoing claim against the RAF about contracting cancer and he asked me to check through his legal documents. In black and white, it said that he had multiple myeloma and that life expectancy was ten years. He'd been diagnosed in 2013 and it was now 2018. I tried not to read into it – my sensible lawyer head told me that. Of course, you put the worst scenario in a letter of claim, but the words, the scary sentences, were still there. I couldn't help but think, if our relationship went further, *What would I be signing up for?*

I didn't know if he wanted a friend, a mother for his children, someone to see him through or all three – and I got scared. I wasn't getting the spark even though he was an incredible person, and I needed to be an adult about it, I didn't want to waste his time especially if he didn't have much left. He deserved more. Just before Christmas, I told him all of this but we carried on being friends. On New Year's Eve, Zach had his kids and I invited them all to my party as friends – that carried on, with sometimes a little more that reverted straight back the following morning – and then he started to be here more and more. I still couldn't commit.

When, one day, he told me that someone at the gym had asked him to go for a drink, I said, 'You should go!'

He looked at me and replied, 'You know how I feel, I can't do this any longer. You know how I feel about you. I can't keep waiting and hoping. If you can't give more, I have to say, we're done. I'm done.'

I just thought, *That's rude! He's dumping me and we're not even dating!*

However, at that moment, I also felt something else. I looked at him and knew I had to let someone in. He was so kind and lovely, he was different from all the other ones out there, and I realised I had to knock a few of the bricks out of my wall.

'How dare you!' I said. 'We're *so* not done!'

'But if we're going to date, I want it to be real. I want you to hold my hand when we walk down the street. Can you do that? If you're in, you're in.'

The following day, we went for a walk with Elizabeth. Zach asked her, 'Do you both want to stay at my house tonight and we can watch some Harry Potter?' Honestly, that evening gave me something, the magnitude of which he'll never know. It was the first night I had felt like I had a sliver of normality with love around me again. He was fussing over my little girl, he settled us in his bed together while he slept in a bunk bed; we had the loveliest sleepover. I felt like I could breathe for a little bit. Just being in that environment away from everything, the three of us, was so special.

The following week, he came round one evening and was playing with Elizabeth when she turned to him and said, 'Zach – will you and Mummy be girlfriend and boyfriend?' That was lovely - and it was easy coming from a six-year-old. She always said to me, 'Daddy would want you to be happy and not alone,' and now she was confirming that.

The wife of my dad's brother had passed away the year after the boys. Uncle Ralph had met someone else and they got married in the September of 2019. I saw them together and there was the realisation that it was OK to form another bond. It doesn't replace anything, it never will, but it is fine. You're allowed. We went to the wedding and Zach was really integrated into my family from that point on. It wasn't a big deal, he just fell in. I think that event let me see that love could happen again.

We'd hired a motorhome for us to travel with his boys and Elizabeth. One night in Brecon, it was so hot that we just couldn't sleep indoors. Zach and I took blankets outside so that we could sleep under the stars. As I lay there, safe with him, safe in his arms, I finally felt that I could allow myself that.

'I love you,' he whispered. 'I've never loved anyone before. But I love you.' That made it a little easier for me because, when I worried whether I was giving him enough, I could hold onto that. I was giving him something he'd never had before.

From that point, he started to say, 'I'd really like to marry you.' He actually asked my dad for my hand in marriage before he asked me. He was far from subtle!

'IF you were getting married, IF I was going to propose, IF that was happening, what sort of ring do you think you'd like?' he asked me.

'Well, IF that was going to happen, I'd have to go look at them!' I laughed.

I found this most beautiful ruby ring which seemed perfect as the red symbolised Fraser but Zach was concerned that it was second-hand.

'Doesn't that bother you?' he asked.

'Well, I'm second-hand! I'm pre-loved, aren't I? It seems right to me.'

A couple of days later, Zach suggested a trip to Castell Coch. He knew how much it meant to me given that the animation had been there, and he went down on one knee in a room where we were alone. Honestly, I couldn't have asked him to be more kind, thoughtful or generous. And I felt the boys were there. I felt that Stu and Fraser were watching on, and they were happy for me, they really were. I'd already been through so much of the self-questioning, feeling guilty that I was even considering being with someone else, but I could give myself to the happiness of that moment.

LIFE: A STORY OF BELIEVING

When I spoke to Father Irving about it, he had the perfect response yet again. 'I'm so pleased for you. I always think that the biggest compliment a widow can give to her previous husband is to remarry as they have helped to show them how to love.' It was such a lovely thing to say and helped me reconcile so much. Stu had shown me that movie love that I had been told didn't exist, and now he was showing me that I deserved to keep being loved. I had someone who would put me first again. Did I deserve that? Probably not because some people never get it once. Why should I get it twice? I knew that I had been blessed to have both Stu and Zach in my life, whereas some people don't get anything like that love at all. I didn't want anyone to have the pain I went through but I wish they could have the good stuff – and I was finally coming round to accepting that maybe I could have it too.

The wedding was planned for the May of 2020 but things were about to take a turn that none of us could have expected.

Chapter Twenty-Two

A Marriage

In February, we were in full pelt with all the organisation of the wedding and then, at half-term, I got really ill. I couldn't even get out of bed and I now suspect that I had Covid, which was just starting to trickle through the news - something that was happening abroad, not something that would affect us all here in the UK.

Zach wasn't staying with me officially but he was here a lot, and that helped so much because it meant I had someone to help with Elizabeth for the first time. I remember him taking her to the Big Pit which is a rite of passage being Welsh! I was so annoyed that I couldn't be there to make memories with her, but I was really poorly – I eventually went to the GP and admitted, 'I'm in a bad way, I admit I'm depressed. I don't know if this illness is my mind over my body or my body over my mind because I just can't get out of this. I don't know what's happening.'

Zach had medical health cover with his job which meant that the GP could refer me to someone quickly for therapy but also said that I needed to consider anti-depressants, which I'd never taken, nor had I had treatment for PTSD. The first stop was a psychiatrist and I had to tell my story all over again and listen to him saying, 'I don't know how you survived,' as usual. He didn't even give me the option of anti-depressants, he just decided. I was so ill, I just followed orders.

'I feel incredibly guilty,' I told him.

'Guilty for what?'

'Living. I feel guilty for living. I feel guilty for being with Zach. I feel guilty for having Elizabeth. I feel I don't deserve anything.' At the heart of it was that Stu didn't have her. Some of the angers I had – which I sometimes still do – are that Stu has Fraser but I had Elizabeth and I had two stepsons coming and I was living. I was living. I was smiling a little bit more, I had things in my life.

'You have survivor guilt,' he said, 'and survivor guilt doesn't happen as people think it does. It happens when you do get that glimmer of happiness, that's when it comes.' I'd obviously seen survivor guilt in the organ recipient community, but this was the first time anyone had suggested it applied to me.

I've never been scared of dying. For years, I'd thought it would have been easier if I'd been hit by the car too; if we'd all died. I honestly don't think Stu would have coped if it had just been me and he was left with the kids. He was such an emotional man and

I don't think he would have been able to get through. It was too big. If the four of us had gone together, maybe that would have been better. Even in my darkest days, I could never have thought of Elizabeth being the only one left.

That psychiatrist opened up my mind and also a bit of my heart – *OK, I have survivor guilt,* I accepted, *and I can reconcile that I'm poorly because this is how it's coming out. I'll take the anti-depressants. It's OK to not be OK.*

Covid hit the UK soon after and we went into lockdown. I didn't get on with the anti-depressants as I felt like they made me cross, angry; I had memory loss and I didn't last on them for very long. But worse than that was what happened to Zach. When Covid swept the world, he became so poorly. No one was really able to give positive confirmations of it at the time unless people were hospitalised. There were no lateral flow tests being given out back then; there were no immediate options to get a negative or positive, and all I could see was that he was very, very ill. We didn't know what to do. All that was being shown in the media was people dying. He had moved in and I'd suddenly started being happy again but now, not only did he have cancer, but he possibly had Covid too while he was on the most vulnerable list. I had to just deal with it – again.

One day, it all came to a head. I rang 111 and waited for an hour before they cut me off, meaning that I had to call 999 as I was terrified. They said they'd send paramedics when they could – it was so busy at that stage that they had no idea when that would be.

'You might need a ventilator. You might need to go to hospital,' I told him.

The only person I could talk to was Zach's mum. His dad has a similar condition and I knew that she would have advice.

'If the paramedics are coming, how are you going to deal with that?' she asked me.

It suddenly hit me. How would I do it? Paramedics and an ambulance coming to our house, our place of safety – we'd be thrown straight back into it. I couldn't get in an ambulance, I just couldn't get in the back of one knowing the last time I'd done that had been with Fraser. I couldn't even face seeing an ambulance. These wouldn't be normal paramedics, they'd be masked up due to Covid just as they'd been in intensive care. Elizabeth would see that, let alone the worry that Zach could die, he really could. I'd rather it was me who had Covid, as usual, I would *always* rather it was me. I was completely alone, I couldn't ask anyone to come round as no one was allowed in the house.

But I did cope. I just did.

I kept Elizabeth in the lounge. Zach was upstairs in the bedroom and we'd all been staying apart with me talking to him from the landing. He was being so stubborn, he hadn't even wanted me to call 999, but I had to force this, I had to make sure he had treatment if that was what he needed. The paramedics arrived and, thankfully, they didn't look as bad as I expected. As the days and weeks went on, and stories came out about PPE shortages, I realised that was why they didn't have as much on as I had dreaded - they simply didn't have supplies. They checked everything they could from the front door - they weren't allowed to come into the house - then rang the hospital for advice. Elizabeth stayed in the lounge the whole time and didn't even realise they were there whereas I knew I was in fight mode.

The paramedics decided to risk coming in to do an ECG which helped calm me down emotionally as having another two people there who knew what they were doing helped. They checked Zach thoroughly and then said, 'It's riskier for him to go to hospital – given everything that's going on, he's better staying here with you keeping a close eye rather than perhaps exposing him to anything else.'

Zach pulled through, but I don't think I was prepared for just how hard it hit me when I knew I'd have to face up to paramedics and ambulances again. As soon as we got out of lockdown, we spent most of our time in a caravan in Brecon so that Zach could get better, but I was having to deal with the emotions it had unleashed in me. It was impossible to get any appointments, and I just couldn't access a psychiatrist. The whole country was different and I had no one to talk to, no one to help me through and the message was, 'Everyone is going through the same thing, everyone is struggling.'

I remember having this moment when I said to Father Irving, 'Everyone can see my world now. Everyone can see that the world can alter overnight – it can alter in a second. When they talk about going back to normal, what they don't understand is that you can't go back to normal. That normal isn't there any more. Your life is linear, not circular – you can learn from what's happened in the past, but you can't go backwards.'

I'd known it since that night and now other people were coming to that conclusion too. You just can't go back, you need to progress with that way as best you can. It was un-Christian of me, but I must be honest; I thought that maybe now people could understand a little of what it was like to have life suddenly turned upside down now. My world had been through such things four years ago, and everybody just cracked on; now, on top of my life changing like that, it was getting turned upside down again and I wasn't getting any help when I had admitted I needed it. I just felt incredibly lonely. I felt like I'd been brave to even ask for help and now it wasn't there.

I actually found a lifeline through 'Help for Heroes' who were incredibly supportive about Zach. They had a group called 'Healing Hands' and they provided me with a counsellor. I'd never been more grateful for someone that I could talk to independently and help me through that period. I rang them from the caravan whenever I needed which had become my happy place. I could walk the dog, it was isolated, it was just what I needed. I came off the antidepressants which had never really helped anyway and we stayed in the caravan as much as possible.

On top of that was our upcoming wedding which couldn't possibly happen the way we'd planned it now that Covid was everywhere. From that, came ever more guilt. By delaying it until the following Easter, I had a little more time. There were so many emotions swirling around and it ended up helping hugely. We'd planned to be married on 29th May 2020 in Castell Coch, a blessing in St Martins, then a reception in Dyffryn with over 200 guests. Father Irving suggested the Bank Holiday in August for that.

I had to get the wedding certificate and at the Cardiff Registrar's Office, they asked for Stu's death certificate. I handed over the Coroner's Report and the probate.

'That's not it. That's not enough,' I was told. 'You need a proper death certificate. Where's that?'

I'd never had one.

'Well, I'm here – can you issue that?' I asked. I was on my own with this. Zach lived in a different county and was organising his side of things.

'Yes, if you pay us, we can do that now.'

Shaking, I waited.

'No, you can't have that,' the woman said when she returned after ten minutes or so. 'He didn't die in Cardiff, did he? He died in Rhondda Cynon Taf.' I had to make an urgent appointment to go there and obtain Stu's death certificate to allow me to get married. Again, it was another memory, it was another knife in my heart. I'd never seen the death certificate before – the Coroner's Report was worse. On a day when I was meant to be happy, when I was meant to be moving on to the next stage of my life, I was still being dragged back and reminded that I was where I was.

Even though you're starting a new chapter in your life, it's not new is it? You still have to take your past with you.

My friend Michelle came with me because going to Rhondda Cynon Taf meant going back to where Stu had died. It was another horror that I just had to get through. Sometimes I feel like I'm watching someone else doing all of this rather than think about the fact that it's me and I definitely had that sensation on that day.

Zach and I had a virtual wedding on the 29th May due to Covid, and rearranged the actual physical one for Easter the following year; however, Zach became concerned about a second lockdown so we changed it to 30th August 2020. We got married in St Martins and had the reception in our garden instead. It seems surreal to look back on all of that now. I'd ordered a second-hand dress from Cancer Research, which seemed appropriate, but I couldn't get it fitted due to lockdown so I got a John Lewis off-the-rail one instead. It was actually all a relief. I didn't have any of the pressures of who to invite and who not to invite because it was restricted anyway. I'd got to the point of thinking, *Well, if people don't like what I'm doing, that's fine, because there's nothing I can do about it.*

We were going to set up a marquee in the garden for our reception and, in it, we could have thirty people at a time – we went for two sittings. There would be one in the afternoon who would then leave and another thirty would come in for the evening 'session'! I had to have hand sanitisers everywhere, a cleaner in between both groups of people, and even arrows for a one-way system inside the marquee. I was constantly 'doing' something and that's what I needed. I'll do anything to divert from thinking or feeling; it's dissociation, and I even did it on my wedding day.

I loved that it wasn't a spectacle, it was something absolutely perfect for what we needed. I wrote a speech that said all the right things, and I paid homage to the boys in it. By doing that, I do think I was justifying my behaviour in marrying again and therefore I had to ensure if there was anybody who was watching or listening, I got my point of view across that Zach was not replacing Stu. I needed – and still need – people to know that you can grieve and love at the same time.

I used the words of AA Milne to tell Zach what he meant to me – I got my inspiration from another bear that day! Zach was Piglet and I was Winnie the Pooh being told, 'You're braver than you feel.' That's what he'd done – he allowed me to put some wellies on and dance in the rain. That hadn't stopped my feeling that I need to constantly justify myself, that I always feel people are thinking or saying, 'Well, she recovered quickly, didn't she? She moved on.'

It's exhausting and I wish I didn't care. If I could talk to myself, I'd say, *Stop justifying everything you do, stop caring what other people think, you do often make the right choices – be kinder to yourself because you wouldn't be like this with anyone else.* I wish I could. I wish I could ease some of this pain because I just can't. I never stop feeling like I'm letting myself down and I have no idea how to change it.

I don't know how people get to not caring about things. I'm still a child who needs that constant reassurance that I'm doing OK. I'm a grown woman who has accomplished things so why do I need this constant reminder than it's all fine? Maybe it's partly because life keeps getting in the way.

At Easter 2021, my uncle Ralph was diagnosed with bowel cancer, which was the same time I was referred for EMDR. By June, Ralph was told that he had a month to live – that was the first time I'd maybe had to truly face up to the fact that Zach was living with cancer. I'd largely followed his lead up until that point and buried my head in the sand. He wasn't receiving treatment and sometimes we were able to forget, but when Uncle Ralph was diagnosed, it had to be processed.

That summer, we took Dad to see Uncle Ralph, basically knowing it was to say 'Goodbye.' That hit me – how do you do this? How do you actually go and say goodbye to someone? I had never done that before and I'd never had it with Stu and Fraser. But how do you actually do it? With Uncle Ralph, it wasn't about me, it was about my dad and I needed to look after him as he had been my rock, my support, through all of this. His love and pride never faltered and this was the least I could do, but I knew that my own loss, my own history was trying to break through all the time.

When we were there, Ralph got a call to say that he had to go to hospital immediately for a blood transfusion, so that meant we didn't need that big, final goodbye – and, actually, he held on until October. I had this overwhelming guilt that I hadn't gone in to see the boys in the funeral director and it came back when Dad went to see his brother. I could justify it as they looked so peaceful when I'd had to leave them both in the hospitals but I still think, *How could I not?* But how could I have either? Would I now be having flashbacks to seeing them?

I couldn't go to Uncle Ralph's funeral. I was incredibly ill, no doubt because Ralph was the first person I was close to who had died since the boys had passed. My body was screaming at me again to listen, to pay attention but, again, the guilt kicked in. I was terrified I would fall apart and that wasn't my right, that wasn't my place. Who would I be crying for? Myself? The boys? Uncle Ralph? What if I didn't get it right? What if I completely fell apart and people thought I was making it about me? It took everyone else to make me see that I physically couldn't go. I needed someone else to make that decision.

A few days after the funeral, Zach and I went to see Ralph's widow, Sue. It had been their wedding that had shown me that finding love again is a possibility. It hit me that she had nursed two husbands through cancer and I got scared. I really missed Uncle Ralph but how would I do this for Zach? She had lost twice, she allowed love to come into her heart again, and she said that at least she'd had four good years with him – but that's not fair. I felt and knew her pain so much. I started with a new therapist after that but the anticipatory grief was there all the time - I was so scared and I *am* so scared. If I lose him, how will I deal with that?

It made me realise that you need to grab every moment, you need to make memories – but I'm terrified that grief is coming. I knew from the start that Zach had cancer and I committed to him, but it's hard to mesh those two things together. The easiest way is to say, Zach could get hit by a car tomorrow – and I know the consequences of that, don't I? The only bit we do know is that we *don't* know what's coming. We certainly didn't know when we went to that party that we'd be half a family by the following day and I don't know what the future holds either.

You can only live for the moment and I need to grasp that in my hands every single day. And if there was ever a person that encapsulated that feeling, it was a little boy called Roman.

He was the recipient of Fraser's heart.

Chapter Twenty-Three

A Shared Heart

London was deserted.

The city should have been bustling but it wasn't. It resembled a film set where everyone had finished for the day, with just a few workers left scattered here and there. The Christmas decorations were up, but silently twinkling for no one. Covid had wiped out the festive season.

We had come to see Roman. In the weeks leading up to the trip, Zach had thankfully managed to recover from Covid. But following that scare, there were plenty of social media posts outlining plans for Roman going into hospital too. That was now my new worry. As usual, I went inside myself, shielding in my own thoughts. I had this complete panic. I already knew that one of Fraser's recipients had passed away and I now knew where his heart had gone. Therefore, I would know if Roman didn't make it. How would I deal with that? Would I feel as if I'd lost Fraser again?

In the weeks leading up to our London trip, I couldn't stop looking at Zoe's Facebook page. It was somewhat like scratching a constant itch. It was a form of self-harm, but it was also giving me a bit of feeling through the numbness I often experienced. I could see Roman being tested; I could also see that he was so vulnerable, and I understood it all because I was living it with Zach. Covid had seemed to pass somewhat, and summer had made everything a bit better. A few years prior to this, I had received a Christmas present from Roman. It was a picture, in a frame, a rainbow of thumbprints of his entire class, with those of him and his twin brother at the bottom. Something about that hit me hard and a few months later, I had said to Dad and Zach, 'I think I want to meet Roman.'

Dad said he would go to London with me, but Mum disagreed with that. In reality, I didn't need him. Zach could come if I had to have someone there, but Dad was adamant that he wanted to be there himself. Zoe, her partner, and Roman, were coming down from Hartlepool for one of their trips to Great Ormond Street Hospital and I suggested that we had a meal at the Rainforest Café, which the charity agreed to organise. It was going to be quite overwhelming for all of us, there was no doubt about that, but I hoped there would be some distractions for the kids there.

Dad and I went to London on the train and that was when he asked me questions about Roman and his family. At that point, I knew quite a bit through social media, and I went through more on the train ride. I understood that Roman had a carer for a lot of his needs and that he was part of a very young family, with a new stepdad and a new little girl since he and his brothers had been born. When we arrived, we walked around Covent Garden which felt surreal – how could London be so empty? It was as if it had all been cleared and prepared for me to go on a stage and meet Roman. We got to the area where the Rainforest Café is quite early and decided to go for a drink. When Dad went to the loo, I took my phone out. This was a moment I needed to document, just like Stu had documented everything. All I could do was tell myself how I felt, what I was getting ready to do, and how I didn't really have any idea about what was going to happen. I felt I had to do that for Stu as much as for myself.

Dad and I walked over to meet Zoe just as they were walking towards the entrance at the same time, but from the opposite direction. That was the best way it could have happened. It wasn't contrived, it was like we had just bumped into old friends. Roman was in a wheelchair but he hopped out immediately when he saw me and gave me a high five.

It was easy. It felt natural. I could breathe.

We went in, with Zoe and her partner Ryan, and I felt she was really relaxed. Now that I know her a bit more, I understand that nerves were making her quite subdued at the time, but it looked like she was doing well. It struck me how very young they were and how much they had to cope with. Roman had a tracheotomy and was peg-fed, and I felt so guilty that we'd brought them somewhere to eat, but I hoped he would get some pleasure from everything that was going on. They sat across from us and it became clear that Ryan was an absolute star. He was the 'outsider' as it were and was very chatty so that the four of us could just work out what to do, and that was a breath of fresh air.

Roman was a very poorly boy but I didn't really see him in that way. I did worry he would be lost through Covid, and I thought I hadn't properly grieved for Fraser. I worried that when his heart stopped, would that be the moment when it would hit me that my bear had truly gone? It was maybe worrying about Roman in a selfish way and that cut me up, but I managed to not think of that when we were there. The biggest compliment that Fraser could have for his gift would be that the recipient lived life to the max and I could see that this little boy was brimming with enthusiasm for everything, even though he'd been through an incredible amount already in his life.

Roman knew who I was and he knew that he had my little boy's heart. Zoe had obviously done with him what I'd done with Elizabeth and treated him with respect, giving him the information he needed in an appropriate way. I was overwhelmed to be honest. As the meeting continued, understanding what they had been through just blew me away. Maybe I didn't even fully comprehend it at that point. I think now of whether Zoe has survivor guilt and whether sitting there across from me, knowing that my son had to die to give her son a chance at life, was hard for her.

Hearing about their day-to-day struggles was a shock. Roman needed a kidney but he wasn't strong enough to go through it yet. I had learned through my dealings in the transplant world that if you do get a heart, you probably will need another organ, but it was still hard to look at that little boy and think that he required even more. Roman needed daily dialysis which was also an enormous undertaking. It meant Zoe committed her whole life to him. As a mother, she always had to put Roman first and I could see that so clearly. I was in awe of what she had done - to have the bravery to have more children was incredible.

Later in our friendship, I found out that it had been suggested she terminate Roman because of his condition when she was pregnant. I hadn't known that. She'd fought for his life just as I'd fought for Fraser to go to Bristol but already I could see that she was an absolute warrior for him. Before I met Zoe, I worried that I would subliminally wonder if Roman deserved to have Fraser's heart. I worried that I might have that feeling, although un-Christian and hard to admit, which made it a sheer relief to know that he deserved it so very much. That family shouldn't have to deal with what was ongoing for them. I felt at that point that he may have Fraser's heart but I needed to do even more, I needed to help more. They'd had such a struggle and it wasn't going to end any time soon.

Roman was such a sweet boy and needed to be recognised as the amazing fighter he is. I wanted to fix everything for them. Maybe that distracted from how hurt I was – if I could fix everything for everybody else, that would be good, even if I couldn't be fixed. I ached to help them.

After a while, Ryan said, 'Go on – show Anna what you've done.' Roman took off his coat. 'He designed this last night, he wanted to do this for you.' Roman had a football shirt on and a sign on it that this was for his donor. He had a printed-out picture of the animated bear on the front and 'FAB' on the back with the number 7. 'It was all him,' Ryan told me.

That was the only time I cried.

It was so clear straightaway how amazing Ryan was with him and how Roman adored his stepfather. I felt that reflected my relationship with Zach and how incredible he was with Elizabeth. I knew Stu would be glad that I had someone beside me and that Elizabeth had Zach's influence in her life. I could see that reflected with Ryan and Roman.

'Come and see the fish,' I suggested to Roman when he got scared by the artificial thunderstorm that comes every so often in the Rainforest Café. When that happened, he went from this very emotionally intelligent, mature child to a vulnerable little boy. He voluntarily took my hand and I lifted him up to look at the tank. His mum could understand what he was saying but I couldn't, so I just asked him questions such as 'Which one looks like me? Which one reminds you of your mum?' A couple of times when he was in my arms, I had to look away; I couldn't let him see I was upset. I didn't want him to feel this was a day of sadness, it was more of an emotional release for me.

When I was holding him, I didn't feel his heart but I was holding him like my bear – in a bear hug. For me, it was about the whole person, not just a heart. Beforehand, in my head, he had my bear's organ, he had his heart and that did sometimes freak me out that Fraser's heart was beating when he was no longer here. When Roman was there, it felt that Fraser was there too. From the showing of the shirt and then feeling the connection with the fish, I felt it. When we went back to the table, Roman came and sat on my dad's lap. It was more beautiful than I could ever have hoped; I hadn't imagined just how special it would be. It was relief too.

Zoe then explained that Roman liked to play air guitar. That was bizarre – none of his family was musical at all, but he loved to do it. 'I see a lot of your social media posts and I think, *That's like Roman*,' she said. Time kind of ran away from us and we had to get our train back. I said to Roman, 'I promised I'd buy you a toy. What would you like?' He did the typical child thing of checking everything out and I was a little worried about missing our train home! He decided on a gorilla and then the following day a memory came up on my Facebook of Fraser and a gorilla toy. The exact same one that Roman had chosen!

From that point on, Zoe and I communicated a lot. I decided on the way back that I would message Rebecca, the journalist who had done the original story on Zach's cancer. She rang me almost immediately to check that I'd give them the story of us meeting. It was like a whirlwind. She said that, as they were still in London at Great Ormond Street Hospital getting tests, could I get back there on the Friday? I could if it meant getting this story out there in a way that would work for all of us. All of a sudden, I was back on this wheel that I couldn't stop. Zoe said, 'Roman will be really excited having a photo shoot, and I'm getting my hair and make-up done!' It was good that they were getting a bit of attention I felt, but I had a feeling of dread that it was all starting again.

I took Elizabeth with me and to see her engaging with Roman was amazing – they were playing pat-a-cake games and connected with each other beautifully. To her, it was normal and she took it all in her stride. She became the big sister in a way with him; she was very maternal.

Roman had to get daily dialysis as he only had one kidney and had done so through the whole London trip as well. If he did get a kidney, it would be very risky for him to undergo that operation due to his current state and his fragility. The doctors were saying that, because he coped so well with the dialysis three or four hours a day, and you can live with kidney disease, it wasn't something he absolutely had to have immediately. Zoe took him to hospital for the dialysis every day and her whole world revolved around him.

Everybody in the family had to be trained in peg feeding in case they looked after Roman, but nobody wanted that responsibility, so everything fell on Zoe, with another three kids to look after too (Pixie, her baby girl with Ryan, a five-year-old, and Roman's twin). They decided they were going to leave Roman on dialysis for as long as they could in the hope that he would get stronger for the operation to be done at less risk. That was the best option for them at that moment. What would any of us do in that situation? I think I'd do exactly the same. I would do whatever I could for my son.

Zoe messaged me two days after we did the interviews. 'They asked me for a photograph I'd taken at the time of the transplant with Fraser's heart,' she told me. We always called it Fraser's heart, not Roman's heart. Due to the size of Fraser's heart and because Roman was only eleven months old, it was placed into him and they had to have almost clingfilm over the top for constant watching. 'I'd only ever kept that photo for me,' Zoe said. 'I wanted to ask you before I allow them to publish it – would it be OK?'

I remember thinking, *This is really nice that she's checking with me.*

I messaged her back saying, 'Maybe you can let me see it before I agree or not?' I was in the process of typing, 'but let me know before you send it so that I can get myself in a place where I'm ready to see it.'

Whilst I was typing it, Zoe sent the photo.

That's the photo I wish I'd never seen.

'Thank you for checking with me – no,' I had to say.

That wasn't a photo anyone needed to see.

It was so medical, it was so overwhelmingly medical. I went into protective mode. I wanted to protect Zoe, Roman, Elizabeth, me, everyone – no one needed the vision of what I saw. No one needed to see Roman's chest wide open with Fraser's heart in there. I was just incredibly relieved that Zoe never did disclose that. Even when she did stories before we were in contact with each other, Zoe never allowed that photo to be made public. I was so grateful. It's hers, she could have done whatever she wanted with it and, actually, although we speak of Fraser's heart, this was Roman's heart now. She was respectful enough to check and that meant the world to me.

Zoe and I began talking and opening up a lot more. We started Facetiming a lot although we were very quiet over the anniversaries. We then had the call to invite us onto *This Morning*.

'I cannot do this over the anniversary,' I told them.

About a month after we'd met in London, I realised I wasn't doing too well. When I fell apart in January, Dad told me it was because I'd met Roman, but for me it was because the circle had been completed a little and I'd allowed myself to fall apart as I could see something conclusive - he'd reached his seventh birthday. His story made me reflect on my story.

I don't believe I went through denial, anger, bargaining, acceptance, or anything like that. Maybe it hit me so hard as I was moving towards acceptance. The denial is often my safety blanket which draws me back, and acceptance is the hardest stage which is why it takes so long to get there. Meeting Roman had maybe moved things a little forward for me in terms of processing everything. It made me look at aspects of my life and question them a little deeper. It also brought me to the idea that my story had to be told.

There is some suggestion now that there is a sixth stage of grief and that stage is telling your story, allowing others to bear witness to your trauma. There is something in that. I struggled with this as I felt it was egotistical to do this. Other people might say it's brave; I don't see that. I don't need to protect anyone or anything any longer - I need to actually bear what happened, otherwise what is the point? I've learned so much writing this all down. It's taken me on an emotional rollercoaster. Stu would hate me saying that - he always got so annoyed at anyone on 'X Factor' who said it!

And in a strange way, I often feel I have the luxury that they are remembered separately rather than bound together. When I see anything about the Hillsborough disaster for example, my heart breaks for those families who are all lumped together as 'the 96'. They're not just a number, they're not just one 'thing' – each of them is loved, each of them is an individual.

Falling apart then is perhaps what needed to happen. The process of looking back also awakened me to where I am now and what lies ahead. It is OK to still love Stu even though I'm with Zach. It's OK to love Zach even though I loved Stu. In our wedding vows, I referenced the midwife who told me that when you have a baby, another piece of your heart grows. It's true – and when I married Zach, another piece did grow for him and his children. What I didn't appreciate was it's a different kind of love that I'm getting now. That's fine. You don't have to have the same love for everybody. Yes, I fell in love with Zach, but that wall is there that I have to work on. I have to let him into my heart a little bit more than I do.

Everyone tells me I'm so strong, but that I also need to grieve and not be so focused on the charity, but also strong for Elizabeth. How can you be it all? How can you be strong for your daughter but grieving when it's only the two of you left? Maybe now is the time to grieve and be angry as Elizabeth is more mindful; she is incredibly supportive. She wants to talk more, she wants to know more. To get back to our original need to live for today, not worrying about the future or dwelling on the past.

I never signed up for any of this. I get very upset if people think I was enjoying any of it, the meeting celebrities, the going to LA – this all happened, this awful thing happened, and all I could do was to try and get something out of it. I was lucky that the boys weren't just a number, that their memories were kept alive because of *Believe*, that there were organ donations, that there were conversations, but I didn't sign up to lose my husband and son.

All I knew at the time was that I had a very small window to try and make a difference – how could I use it? I was still trying to do that but there was no denying that some moments were harder than others. This was one of them.

What have I learnt through those moments?

Looking forward, I still have work to do. And it's behind that wall where most of my battles ahead lie.

Chapter Twenty-Four

The Wall

In the years since I lost the boys, I've built up what I call The Wall. It's there to protect me. Or at least, I think it is.

For you, and for anyone else who thinks they know my story, there's the one side of the wall. That's the public face that everyone sees. The 'brave face' that attends events, makes public announcements - even heading out the door to go shopping.

What goes on behind that wall is a different story, however.

I wasn't diagnosed with PTSD until the November after it happened when it should have been clear to anyone that I would be suffering after such a trauma. It felt like every time I went to the GP, I'd be asked if I minded some students sitting in. I never had the strength to say 'no,' and that changed how I could be. I wasn't referred to anyone for months. I had some CBT privately which was tricky because it was so hard to deal with the grief and trauma within a way of therapy that only focuses on the present rather than what brought you to that present. I stopped it as it wasn't really helpful. Grief is such a rollercoaster. Sometimes I have to deal with the flashbacks; sometimes I only need to talk to someone outside of it.

I finally got referred for EMDR (Eye Movement Desensitisation and Reprocessing) which some people have straight after a traumatic event but, actually, you can't really get any support straight away. In fact it's recommended that you don't get any mental health help for six months after a major trauma happens. And that brings me to another thing - the way society puts a timetable on grief. Sometimes, I feel like I'm not allowed to grieve any more. It's been almost seven years now and to society, that should be gone or dealt with. I should have moved on.

Society's view of grief is so prescriptive. And most of it is unhelpful. A bereavement charity recently urged everyone to light a candle to remember the ones we had lost. It made me cross. Who are they to tell me and all of those other people that, at that specific time, we should light a candle to remember our loved one? I find that very difficult – to be afforded the luxury by society and social media to think about my loss at that particular time. That sort of thing just doesn't sit right with me. When the candle has burned away, do I just move on? Has my time for grief been allocated and run out? That sort of thing doesn't help me in any way with my loss. Everyone's loss is different and no one understands what another person is going through; to pigeonhole everyone is insensitive.

Along the way, I've met a lot of mothers who have lost children. It's the club you never want to join, but you do find some comfort together, even if being boxed in with everyone else is too much. I don't want to light a candle when I'm told to, I don't want to be as easily 'sorted' as that as I'll never be sorted, but if I don't like it, then does it appear that I don't care? It's an eternal struggle about what society says or thinks or what they think they're helping you with. There's an Organ Donation Week in September every year. That makes me feel, is this not worthy of discussion on all the other 51 weeks of the year?

Behind the wall, I still talk to the boys every day. I ask Stu for help, I go to the grave. I ask if they're proud of Elizabeth and if I'm doing OK. I still need that constant reassurance from them. Over the years, I've had little signs from them. Whether or not they meant anything, it doesn't matter – they meant something to me. If they helped me through the difficult time, that was the important thing. Two robins used to follow me around the local park. One was much bigger than the other, and I would always take that.

One year, we went away over the anniversary of the deaths, on a Caribbean cruise. On the 5th, we were in St Kitts and I took Elizabeth swimming with dolphins as I'd done that with Fraser – she actually hated it! Two days later we docked in St Martin, which is the same name as my church. Dad and I planned to go to the local church to light candles. I'd got into doing that a lot and I think it stemmed from the open day after the boys died when everyone was lighting candles. I do that wherever I am - I always find a church and light candles for them. Anyway, when we got there, a mass was going on, which was strange as it wasn't a weekend, it wasn't a Sunday. After we lit the candles, I said to Dad that we should stay for the mass and a hymn started. I couldn't believe it when this wonderful black gospel singer began singing *Bread of Heaven*. That was such a Welsh song and, not only that, it was a hymn at our wedding. It's not an advent hymn and that was another sign – a few days after our wedding anniversary and also around their death anniversary.

Behind the wall can be lonely. I'm never afraid of happiness, I'm afraid of sadness, crying, longing, grieving and the loneliness. I'm terrified of being fragile. I'm scared I'm going to break. Everybody, me included, thinks I'm Teflon. If I did break, I don't think I would ever be put back together again. That brings such fear for me and Elizabeth. If I broke, I have this worst-case scenario that I will suddenly lose my mind and I'll be put in some kind of institution or locked up in some Jane Eyre-esque attic. It just feels like I can't let that script unfold, I can never lose my mind because of the sadness. That's what I'm most scared of.

I have parameters around how I allow myself to think of Stu and Fraser. I can grieve, I can cry, I can still talk to them but I can't go beyond a certain point. Sometimes that is for myself, sometimes I use the excuse that it's for other people; that I'm not allowed to sit and dwell because you've got to get on, and life is about moving forwards and they wouldn't want you to be sad, and therefore . . . I even hear it from Elizabeth.

'They wouldn't want you to be sad, so stop it, Mum.' And where does she get it from? Me probably. She's not just suddenly made that up, she's feeding back to me, so what am I feeding her? I thought it was great showing her to be strong but I need to open up to her more now and say, 'It's OK to be sad, it's OK to miss them. Yes, they may not want us to be sad but we can sometimes feel that way and we can miss them.' When you hear your child talking to you so firmly, telling you not to be emotional, that hits hard. I need to go back and I need to break those walls down to allow me to feel. I've been scared to feel.

I've never allowed myself to feel the complete and utter ache of losing them. I've just plodded on and taken everything as it comes, as that has been the only way through it. I've escaped many times, I've run away every anniversary. I run away and I still manage to do something, as in I never just run away and be me. I've always got the bear wherever we are, and that is the guilt part of me. Am I allowed to feel? Do I deserve to feel? Do I deserve to be sad because they can't? I think I feel like I must have done something for it to happen. It's all related round telling Stu not to drive. I can't help it. I hate when someone says I'm being brave or strong or they could never deal with it if they were me because it makes me a better person than I feel I am. That's why I struggled even starting this book as it feels really, I don't deserve anybody to feel sorry for me. I don't deserve empathy, I don't deserve praise, I don't deserve accolades because I must have done something to deserve this.

I also don't think this is God's will. I do think God is kind, and He and the boys are here to guide me through it but I think this is where I just don't know. I would never say the things to my worst enemy that I say to myself. What I do with the charity, what I do with everything is, I say to people, I'm not telling them what to do, there's no judgement, everybody deals with everything in different ways, everybody deals with death in different ways. I say that to everybody else, but still, I can't say that to myself.

Opening up with this book is the hardest thing, apart from losing them, that I've ever done. It's taken so many chapters to even properly open up. There's Anna-Louise over there, she's won a 'Pride of Britain' award, she's brave and strong, she gets through every day, she has managed to get her daughter to school every single morning since it happened – and hasn't broken down at all. Well, yes she has. Yes, she has but you haven't seen it. Because it all happens behind The Wall.

An hour talking to someone doesn't break those walls down. You have to get back on the treadmill after an hour with a therapist after six, seven years of building that wall. It didn't start as a fully sized wall either – I've added to it over the years. Even if I had a magic time machine and I could go back and speak to myself following the funeral, I couldn't change it. I had to have that head on to cope.

When people say, *I couldn't cope the way you cope, I couldn't deal with it, I'd crumble*, that doesn't help. It turns me into something 'other'. I have to live up to that, I can't take the walls down, I have to keep going. They make me live up to that expectation. When people trot out those clichés, I think, *you don't know how you would cope.* You don't think, how could you ever think this is how you would deal with things? You don't think this would ever happen in the first place. All I've done is build that wall up around myself. I surrounded myself with people who didn't act or deal with my pain because that was the easiest thing. You don't have to be the better person because being the better person stinks actually. You're a better person if you just let yourself *be* yourself.

I feel blessed to have had that amount of time with that love. Some people never get it. When I'm in a more positive mood, I do think about that gift of love I was given. I don't think I computed at that time that they were never coming back. I still struggle. It's taken all these years for me to accept. I don't think I understood how hard it would be to write all of this down, because I've never spoken about the 'after' before. People want to know about the actual day, that's where all their questions lie. If you've read this far, you've shown me that respect at least.

Elizabeth said to me the other day, 'I'm really sorry Mum if I remind you all the time that Daddy and Fraser have died.'

'Babe, you don't remind me – I think about it all the time.'

'But I don't want to upset you.'

'You don't upset me.'

'But I want to take the pain away.'

'You'll never take the pain away – it's happened but you don't remind me. You support me and you help me and that's important.'

It's so hard to think she's feeling that way but also grateful that she's not scared of telling me how she feels, that to me is more important than anything. She did a Mother's Day card in school and when she brought it with my gifts and breakfast in bed, she said, 'Read my card last – not in front of the boys.' She'd written it from Fraser and Daddy too. She's aware as I am about how she doesn't want to make other people feel uncomfortable. It's our loss.

I asked her recently if she would come to the grave with me in the churchyard of where we got married.

'I wish we'd had more time. I wish *I'd* had more time with Daddy and Fraser because I can't remember them very well. I haven't got many memories of them – I would have just liked them for a couple of more years.'

That broke my heart because I've got so many memories but she hasn't and there's nothing I can do about that. I can't magic that up for her, all I can do is make memories for the two of us. I had the luck of having them in my world and now I need to make sure I make the most out of every opportunity for you never know when something like this might happen to you. I don't want people to think I'm enjoying it; it's been thrown at me and it's my duty. It upsets me that people think I'm dining out on this because I would do anything to not be in this position. I put that on myself as I don't think people would say nasty stuff. I can paint on a smile, I can get through it, but I do set myself up for a lot of internal pain. I feel like I'm constantly having to retell my story, everyone wants it, and it's like self-harm.

Ultimately, I think I would have just really liked to have had some alone time to deal with it all. Nobody could give me that as I had a three-and-a-half-year-old who needed her mum. That would have been the magic wand to me. It used to vex me when people would say, 'You need to be strong for Elizabeth.' I wanted to scream, 'What do you think that I'm doing? I haven't once left her, what do you actually think that I'm doing? Are you saying that I'm a bad mum when I've given everything, everything to her?'

But then, I had her – and she was the only thing that I had left. So, when I say that I wanted that magic wand – would I have allowed it? When you've just lost your child, even although you know it's for your recovery, would you leave your other child? I just wanted to sit in my grief. I wanted the time to wail, I wish I'd gone and shouted on the beach. Screamed and cried and got rid of all the hate towards myself. I would have loved to have gone on a retreat, to have just got away, to escape everything that had happened and then come back feeling a little bit healed. I'd like to do that even now. I could go to the beach, I could shout and cry and wail I guess – but I need to know what would happen if I begin allowing the walls to come down? Would the walls begin to crumble at my howls?

I have to just see how I heal.

I have to appreciate life.

I need to feel.

I want to smell coffee, I need to feel pain, I need to feel cold, I need to feel my senses around me again because I've avoided that. I want to feel things in my soul. I want to feel sheer happiness but also pain. I want to stab myself in the arm just to feel it, really feel it, I want to scream pain out of me. I'm numb to so much.

And then there's love.

I do love. I love Zach, but I'm still scared; the wall is still there. With everybody, death will happen. I didn't think it was going to happen like that, to me, and therefore when will it come again? I'm already building that wall up for when it happens to somebody else that I love. But I need to break that wall down to rebuild it in a way that is healthier. That's the next stage of my life. Not being brave and carrying on.

When I look back at those two weeks between the accident and the funeral, I ask myself 'how on earth did I do that? How on earth did that happen?' I do want to shout at that version of 'me' and tell myself to feel it all, but also to tell other people to stop it and *let* me feel these things. Everybody wanted to help which was wonderful of them but this snowball of *Believe* started that I couldn't stop and all of a sudden, it became a great focus not just for me, but for everyone else.

Missing You

STU BATES
WRITTEN BY
NEIL CHARLESWORTH

WISH UPON A STAR   believe

When someone dies, a lot of people don't know what to do or say, but this was something practical they could do and it was a brilliant tool for them. It remains so but it was and is a very lonely place for me to be. I've had some people say that I don't ever open up – I agree it's hard to be around me. I don't actually want to open up and it's easier to freeze people out as I'm so numb anyway. If I do that, they can't hurt me, leave me or be disappointed in me.

I can't get suitable justice for the pain I went through in the hospital. I can't ever forget the questions they asked me. So, what do I do? Add another brick into the wall I've been building for all of these years – and that I'm terrified I'll build forever. Could I even build myself in, never to reappear?

The truth is that I have built up my wall but the EMDR will hopefully help with that. I keep so much in. I safeguard myself and I need to stop it for my own health. I've spent so long protecting myself, behind my wall, that I don't know how to deal with emotions. I really don't. I haven't always been like that. I try and think about how everyone else is feeling but that isn't because I'm being selfless. It's because that's my coping mechanism. I have never dealt with how I feel, I haven't – and that's what this has really shown me. I've acted like a robot because that's what was needed at the time. I feel that I'm stuck like that. I'm too afraid at chipping away at that wall as I'm worried about it all falling down or finding out what's behind it.

What happens then?

Chapter Twenty-Five

Behind The Mask

Can I really change the world for the better? That's a question I often ask myself.

Despite how things look from the outside, my work with Believe has made me question myself in ways I never thought possible. It has been the charity's core purpose that has kept me going, despite the self-doubt and pain that I have been faced with - and continue to be faced with on a daily basis. But is it possible that my vulnerabilities could upend all the good work?

At times, I feel like I'm alone in all of this, and fighting for a better organ donation system can sometimes catch me off guard. In 2022, I had to go to an organ donation conference in Swansea to represent the charity. The conference was specifically looking at brain stem death. I felt so exposed and really didn't want to be there, but, as always, I got my big girl pants on and did it for *Believe*. It was hard to agree to because it brought back all the old questions of whether I should have fought more for Fraser. Almost immediately I was introduced to a woman who was standing in the middle of the room.

'This is Rachel,' said Harry, who was organising everything. 'She's the nurse who was with you in the Royal Glamorgan Hospital.' I wouldn't have known her if I'd walked past her in the street to be honest, but to be faced with that in public, instantly, knocked me for six.

'I've been seeing what you've been doing with the charity and it's wonderful,' Rachel told me, clasping my hand. All I could do was nod and smile – I had no idea what was expected of me. 'That night,' she said quietly, 'it will always be on my mind you know.'

I did my usual response of, 'Oh bless you!' but inside was screaming, *Do you think it will ever leave my mind? Do you think it helps to tell me that?* That quick conversation took my breath away and then it was straight into a lecture listening to people talk about the tests that are done for brain stem death. They started discussing the Archie Battersbee case which had been in the public eye, where the parents of a boy who was on life support had gone to the High Court to appeal the medical decision. The doctors believed the life support should be switched off as there was no chance of the poor boy recovering, but the mother in particular had launched a huge campaign to fight for Archie to be kept alive any way possible.

She had made comments that alleged doctors wanted to 'harvest' his organs and, outlandish as they were, these comments stick in the minds of the public and the speakers were raising the point that it could affect donation rates. They were all discussing it so objectively whereas I wanted to stick my fingers in my ears. The debate went on and on, the talk of brain stem death and testing was unrelenting, and I couldn't help but think, *Hang on – I've got one of my personal friends and supporters of the charity here who knows what I went through; I'm surrounded by nurses who may have been told by Rachel what I'd experienced, and yet no one is getting me out of here?*

Not one of them thought to do that, to even lean over and suggest I went for a coffee until I felt ready to listen. I was nothing more than part of a clinician's textbook; I was a case study. Could nobody in that room think there might be people there who had been through the hell of it?

The disparity therefore between the public face of Anna and the one that struggles every day, is a big one.

After the conference in Swansea, I felt like I had to get away from the charity for a bit, I needed to escape. I told one of my friends how that event had made me feel and a meeting was called. 'To be quite honest,' I admitted, in tears, 'I just don't know how much fight I've got left in me. I know I'll find it, I know I have to find it, but it's all a struggle.' They were supportive but it felt like, again, I was having to be the one who asked for help rather than someone else noticing.

They agreed that there should be a member of staff in place that allowed me to take a sidestep away when I needed to, and I did feel that was a brilliant option and it cleared my head a little bit as we prepared for another visit to LA. I paid for a Fly/Drive trip to Vegas so that we could combine our family holiday with seeing Mike and the animations, who wanted to discuss translating the animation into more languages.

But we weren't going to get there without another drama. Life still throws curveballs – no one who has lost their loved ones is immune to other things happening. About a week before we left, Zach was very poorly and we thought he'd need further treatment. It was actually all up in the air whether we were going as he did think the cancer was back. His consultant said he could go but we still had the worry that he would need further treatment with no guarantee of how that would work out at some point – a point which seemed to be getting closer with every day.

I think that men have to get to rock bottom before they accept that they need help and there is no denying that Zach has so much on his plate. It's been ten years since his original diagnosis and most people need further treatment within ten years, and I did wonder when we got back if he was gearing himself up for some sort of crisis and facing up to what sort of treatment he might need. He'll definitely need another stem cell transplant at some point and probably more chemotherapy. But we have to accept that he's not 32 years old and fit any more, things have changed. That realisation is terrifying.

I was incredibly emotional before I went to LA but I did love it – there is without doubt a guilt when I enjoy things related to the charity and to the boys. It's an eternal struggle and I worry that people are thinking, *She's getting to do all that because they died*. I'd choose them, of course I would choose them over all of it, over any of it. When we got to America, I did manage to breathe that we'd achieved it, and thankfully we were very busy which distracted us, but there was no getting away from the fact that life is cruel and we were there because of what had happened to the boys.

It hit me in the studio in LA that, actually, *Believe* was doing something pretty amazing. Translating the materials into other languages was an immense task, but Mike was behind everything as always, generous and supportive. The new animation idea was something I felt very strongly about. The organ donation rates in many communities are incredibly low, particularly with Black and Asian people. I'd decided that we needed to have everything in Arabic, in Bengali, in a number of languages to try and break down the barriers that stopped people from donating. The main one is a lack of trust in the government. There is a very high rate of kidney disease in the Muslim community and, therefore, a much higher demand for organs. However, there's a very low number of those organs actually coming from Muslim people, and that needs to be addressed. We need to develop trust and I really do feel that *Believe* can play a significant part in that.

I'd spoken before on radio programmes such as 'Voice of Islam' and had been told that the Quran emphasised saving lives in line with belief, and that was what I needed to get across. If I could get the imans on my side, then they could give guidance and people would listen. I knew this was what I needed to get across, and with a knowledge of what every group would relate to, I could do it.

The donation rates did go up for the summer after Covid because there was a general thankfulness to the NHS for what they did and what they put themselves through. I feel it was society's way of saying 'thank you' but it hasn't stayed at that level, and there is also a shortage of donated blood now too. I argued that we need to widen the debate, to look at how we can keep organs at centres for longer so that we can get better matches, and I've been honoured to be included in the consultation group regarding Welsh objectives upon that, leading up to 2030.

LIFE: A STORY OF BELIEVING

At the moment, a transplant occurs within 12 to 24 hours. The organ is literally put on ice and driven at a fast speed to the recipient. There are so many people on the list and getting donations from all parts of the community is vital, which is why I really felt that translating our message into different languages was a hugely important step. Once we have those donations, the conversation can turn to how best to utilise them. Fraser's heart was too big for Roman and if we had better systems in place, he could have got a more appropriate match.

There are so many unanswered questions but I hope that with time, and with more donations as well as developments in the science, no one will be in the position I was. I get infuriated when I hear people say ridiculous things such as the government tries to harvest organs, or that there is a market in them – but maybe that's all coming from a position of fear. It's probably the case that hearts are particularly emotive. One of the benefits of liver transplants is that they can be done in a relatively healthy way as the liver continues to grow, but everyone knows the truth about heart transplants – there's no easy way around that. You can only get a donation for one reason after all, can't you? My mind was going to all of these things while we were in LA, but I had to focus on what we were achieving.

But all of these things - the discussions, the debates, the arguments - they all take their toll on me. On the day I saw the animation, the emotions hit me again and I was pummelled with the most horrendous flashbacks that night. I tried to make myself see why it was happening, talking about the fears and the cause for such a reaction out loud. *This is because I've been talking about it for days, this is because I saw the animation. We've been travelling around, we've been having fun, but this is the purpose of it all. It's why I'm here and I can't shy away from it.* But it wasn't just that. My mind might have been pushing things away but my Facebook wasn't letting me escape – it was the anniversary of the day the driver was sent to prison. And do you know what that made me think? It made me think that I was almost glad I was suffering because I'd been having such a good time up until then, and, as always, I didn't think I deserved that. At least I had a little bit of pain, I told myself, which was ridiculous as the pain never really goes away.

I had been worried that I would fall apart when I was in Los Angeles as it had been so incredibly stressful and emotional with Zach beforehand, as well as any 'big' trip or event regarding the charity throwing up its own worries. But we had a lush time, always keeping busy, which was ideal. It was like seeing the old Zach and I think it did him the world of good to be the man of the family, driving us around and making decisions. Every day was a new adventure and in some ways, I didn't really want to come back as it was the trip of a lifetime. When I did, it all hit me.

As always, there was the eternal struggle, the guilt that we'd been enjoying things which we'd never have experienced if the boys were still here, and on top of that was the relief that Zach had actually managed to go, as well as genuinely engage with everything. Coming back to reality was a shock and I couldn't stop thinking about the fragility of life, which wasn't helped by my dad's best friend dying of a sudden stroke while we were away.

I was really sick on our return and it struck me again how close the link is between mind and body, between the mental and the physical. Your mind often just tells you at some point, 'You're not listening.' It then does something to *make* you listen, whether that's a tummy upset, a migraine, or the loss of your voice. It's almost as if it's saying, 'I'm going to give you physical symptoms to make you pay attention to the fact that something is wrong. You're not listening to your head, you're not listening to your heart, but maybe you'll listen to your body if it actually stops for a little while in one way or another.'

Maybe that's what happens with Zach too – when his body is in a bad way, he has to face the fact that he can't control what the cancer decides to do, but he can look at how it affects him mentally and emotionally. Men tend to feel that they have to be a certain way, leading as head of the household, and shouldering all of the burdens. I feel I've had to do that, it's mostly been me, and that in itself must be hard for him. There is a conflict between what he feels he should be and how he is, and the negative connotations that come from that at times are really hard.

The fact is, I've been here before. Stu was low, Stu lost his job, Stu died – it's all been in my life at other times and I can feel utterly exhausted when it all raises its head again, even though I'm used to it and I understand how bad times work. This doesn't stop me having the fear, being terrified that something's going to happen again and I'm going to have to dig deep once more – how often can you be asked to do that and keep standing?

On the return from LA, I felt like we all needed to catch a break and that just wasn't happening. Just as I had feared, Zach's health took a turn for the worse.

Chapter Twenty-Six

Distractions

*I**Believed in Forever*

In the middle of September, Zach was in a lot of pain as he'd fallen off a boat the week before.

'It's easier when I lie down,' he told me, 'but I'll get it checked out tomorrow I think.'

Elizabeth was starting back at school the next day and when Zach went upstairs to rest, I helped her get ready. She went to bed a little earlier, bursting with excitement and keen to get a good night's sleep. I couldn't settle so watched some telly then got up for an indigestion tablet.

Zach stirred beside me. 'I've got a bit of indigestion too,' he said, 'can you get me one as well?'

As soon as he took it, he ran to the toilet. When I heard him being sick, I thought it had just hit the back of his throat and made him gag. But as I listened from the bedroom, it soon became clear that the vomiting wasn't stopping. It sounded as if he was filling buckets. It wasn't retching, it sounded different. He finally stopped and I went in to see if he was OK.

There was blood all over the floor and what looked like little bits of tissue. I cleaned up as much as I could but I was heaving with it all too. *We can't have both of us down,* I thought. I wasn't able to face cleaning the very last bit and went back to our room where I Googled furiously.

'Zach, you need to ring 999,' I told him. 'I think you need an ambulance. You've lost a lot of blood and we can't risk that with your cancer.'

He was adamant. 'No, I really don't need that. If it makes you feel better, I'll drive myself there to get a quick check though.' He was kidding himself, given that he could barely sit up in bed and there was no way I could leave Elizabeth in the middle of the night to drive him there. The situation made me take matters into my own hands and I rang for an ambulance. I was advised there was an eight hour wait and that I'd be better to get him to hospital myself.

'I wouldn't even be able to get him out of bed, never mind into the car – and I've got a ten-year-old here. What do you suggest I do?' I was told a paramedic might call me before the eight hours were up. I assumed it would be a triage call and that would move us up the ambulance priority list. Was I scared? I just thought, *He's still talking, he's still breathing.* I was completely desensitised and utterly calm. I knew we both needed to rest and just wait for the paramedic's call. I must have dropped off as Zach woke me at 4am to say the ambulance was there. They came upstairs to assess him and quickly determined he needed to go to hospital.

'We don't know how long it'll take you to get into the actual hospital,' one of them warned us. 'We can get you there – but to actually get you inside? That's another matter as the ambulances are all backed up.'

Zach bumped himself downstairs to get to the vehicle; he was too proud to go out on a stretcher. I waited to see him go off and I froze. I just couldn't go to the back of the ambulance and say goodbye. I couldn't physically walk there. It was as if there was a wall between us and I felt such guilt.

I went back to bed and got Elizabeth off to school the next day. I didn't tell her about Zach as I knew it was in her best interests to head off, happy and unworried. Zach texted me that morning to say he had finally got into A&E. I went in and was told he had lost a couple of pints of blood, but it took until 8pm that night to give him a transfusion. When I went in for visiting the next day, he had just been taken down for the camera. Two hours later, he still hadn't had the procedure done. It turned out he'd been fighting the tube with the camera which went down his throat so much that the doctors hadn't been able to perform the tests anyway, and they'd try it again the next day. What he didn't tell me was that they had done a procedure to stop the bleeding as that was still ongoing and at worrying levels.

In the middle of all of this, the Queen died and that made things even more surreal. It was almost as if the whole country felt this most incredible mass grief, which must have been a reflection of their own losses and, in some ways, it helped me. I was with Zach when I got a call from a friend to tell me that the Queen had died, but I was in a completely different, private world for once. Zach had been so ill – he still was – but no one really knew of our trauma as they had something else to focus on. It was odd to juxtapose the two events and to compare it all with what I had been through before.

I'd had that public loss in my own way. When Diana died, I thought the national mourning for that was due to everyone comparing it to what could happen in their own lives without any warning. It was what I would go through with the boys, it was nothing you could predict, but with the Queen we all knew it was coming.

For those first few days after she died, people were saying to me how sad it all was, but I had to cope with what was happening in my own life with Zach. In some ways, it was similar to when the Welsh team came back on the day the driver was sent to prison and their arrival took the sentencing off the front pages. Now everyone else was transfixed by the death of the Queen and the preparations for her funeral. Meanwhile, I was in my own little world again, quietly able to face what was happening without distractions as everyone was looking elsewhere.

Everything was finally sorted out and Zach got out more than a week after his admission, none the wiser as why it had all happened in the first place. And it made me realise that one of the hardest things I've had to deal with recently is the huge amount of anticipatory grief that has hit me.

Life is really challenging and that surprises me, because when the boys were here, I didn't find life a struggle at all. Day-to-day life was fine. Of course, there were worries about my job, about Stu's job, about general things that everyone can dwell on, but there was nothing like my fear that Zach was never going to make it home again. Trying to deal with someone who is incredibly poorly and who has emotions of their own to contend with related to their own health is another layer of worry that I'm not sure I've come across before.

When the boys died, I had no warning. With Zach, it's there all the time, and the hospitalisation brought that home to me in such a harsh manner. When the boys died, I was just dealing with what was in front of me and plodding along. With Zach, there is always a worry that this time might be the end, and I did worry with the bleeding that our time was up. I actually said to myself, *I'm not going to deal with this the way I did last time,* as if I was already writing the script for when I was going to lose my next husband.

We had it in our minds that he got his bloods done every eight weeks to flag problems. If there were any, hospital would be arranged, more tests would be done, but it would all be very controlled. This event had shown us just how naïve we were. Nothing had been picked up in his bloods, the security of the parachute we thought was there had been false all along.

All of this leads me to being scared of the future rather than being able to enjoy the present, but that's my normal; that's my life now. Sometimes it all boils over through the most ridiculous things. Not long after Zach got out, a carton of soup fell from the fridge one day. It didn't even splash open, but I started crying, shouting that life was so hard, and actually feeling a bit of relief that I'd managed to let my emotions out.

Everything with the charity was snowballing at this time too. I was involved in planning a *Believe* memorial garden in Cardiff which was something I had never envisaged. My focus has always been on education and support, but actually, there are so many other things that can be done, there are other ways we can reach people. The garden is planned to be in the grounds of a crematorium. It'll be a reflective space which will encourage people to think about the positives of life rather than loss, and I was delighted to be part of it.

The garden has a flowing design and anyone can go there to pause and to remember. I don't want it just to be about death; I want it to be about the circle of life, about how we all help each other along the way. It will also be a learning garden with educational messages. There will be a heart in the centre which will be viewed from Google Earth next to mounds reflecting the kidneys and liver.

There will be quotes from donor families, a replica of Castell Coch and a tree to honour each organ donor in Wales with a heart attached; nearby, the council's Forget-You-Not Garden, largely to remember people who died during the Covid pandemic. In the centre, there will be a post box where visitors can pick up an envelope, write their message, and post it. They can take away wildflower seeds to plant, or to plant them while they're in the garden. There will be handprints and footprints for people to find their match and these will be of inspirational people connected to Wales but ultimately to show that everyone's journey is ultimately the same. There will be signs of love and hope all around.

And there will be bears. Lots of bears.

All of these things provided a distraction for me at a time when I could have so easily been overwhelmed. While Zach was still recovering, another opportunity arose when I was asked to present a paper at a conference for The Institute of Crematorium Management. Preparing for the event gave me something to focus on, but my worries were never far away. I did packs for all the delegates so that they knew about *Believe* and made sure they each had a bear to take home with them. There were so many people there with their own stories of donation, not all of them positive. I gave my speech and could see tears in the eyes of many delegates, but the main thing I wanted to get over was that no one has to do this alone. Yes, there will be people during the hospital process who will guide you, but when all of that fades, you need more. I want that to be what *Believe* stands for – more in every way.

I left the conference buzzing. I was glad that I'd pushed myself and gone because it gave me a sense of being 'me' again. Maybe that gave me some strength because, soon after, I got a message from Zoe to say that Roman had been in hospital for the past eight weeks and wasn't well at all. The doctors were talking about bringing his transplant forward but having to juggle that with the reality that he was too poorly for the best outcome. It would be a very risky procedure and he was getting even more unwell as time went on. The longer they could keep him on dialysis the better as it would make him bigger and stronger, but the delay could have consequences. We'd all know that this was going to happen at some point, but everyone hoped it would be at a time when Roman was in a better place.

Again, I immediately went into practical mode – what could we do, what could we provide? The emotional side is just too much, and as I've always said, Roman is Zoe's boy; he's not mine and I don't want to be seen as parachuting in with my grief and my past. The truth is, I don't know how I'll feel when something happens to Roman as I've never been through that exact scenario before, so I try to push it away. I tried to think about Roman's twin, a seven-year-old boy who is watching all of this, who must have so many questions and feelings of his own. How could he possibly cope?

When Roman does get his transplant, he'll be in Great Ormond Street Hospital for around three months and I'll do all I can for them during that time. Whatever they want, I'll be there and *Believe* will be there too. When someone is going through that sort of thing, or when someone is going through grief, lots of people say, 'What can I do for you?' That brings an incredible amount of pressure. You have to think of something when thinking is what you're running from.

Don't ask a grieving person what you can do for them as you're asking them to make another decision. Instead of saying those words, specify something – would it help if I did the washing? Can I take the dog for a walk? Would you like me to make some meals for the freezer? They only have to say 'yes' or 'no.' I try to do that with the charity. I give people options of what we can provide rather than force them into thinking of yet another thing, and I did that with Zoe. She would never come out and say, 'I want accommodation for three months,' but if I go and organise that and offer it, that's a different matter and it's the approach that should be taken in practically all situations like this. When people have been through a transplant, they generally think that they've been given the ultimate gift, so how can they possibly ask for anything else, no matter how small? I know that feeling all too well, I hate asking for help too as I should be grateful for the support I've had already. It takes a lot to say, 'well, actually . . .'

When I'd left Fraser, it was about nine or ten o'clock in the evening. The operation didn't happen until lunchtime the following day, and a lot of things can happen, medically, in that period of time. That wasn't explained to me, nor was the possibility that Fraser's heart could be rejected. I do know that one friend told me that she went through all the paperwork and emotion, then her daughter died before the donation process could occur. I wasn't warned that the organs might not be utilised

– but how much of a warning could they give or could I have absorbed?

At that time, in the moment, I would think very little. But afterwards, it's a different story. The support in the time that followed was sadly lacking and I desperately want to change that. To be told that some recipients had passed away took a great deal from me, emotionally. I'd had to make that call anyway; no one offered the information, and not only did I have to face up to the fact that the recipient had died, but I had to grieve again.

The way I tried to look at it was, that person had gained another 18 months they wouldn't have had without Fraser giving them such a precious gift. I didn't get another 18 months with my little boy, and I had to find a reason for the donation to have even happened. I shouldn't have had to do self-therapy though; someone should have been there for me. Perhaps somewhere at some point, it's decided that a line has been drawn under it all. Maybe someone says, 'She doesn't need to be informed any more, she doesn't need anything else from us.' There's no discussion *with* you, but maybe there is *about* you. Maybe I was on the clock, my grief expected to end once a certain time arrived, a time that I didn't know was ticking away. There is no time that is 'easy', no matter how many days, weeks, months, years pass. There will always be something and I'll always be in limbo, still broken over the loss of my Fraser Bear, still knowing that people will be thinking I should have moved on.

What do I do? Where do I go? I don't know. I'll wait for the token texts on the 26th of August and the 15th of September, then on the 6th of December, maybe Christmas Day, maybe my birthday. Those are the five days a year where people remember but the harsh part of me thinks that they've probably just popped a little reminder in their phone calendar or it comes up on their social media. It's not something that's with them or is constantly in their mind. They have to be reminded. Their lives have definitely moved on. I think it's easier for most people not to see me and then they can just focus on their world and everything in it. When I look back at the woman I was before it happened, and the woman I am now, the biggest difference is that my naïvety has gone.

Juxtaposed to this is that I also then feel guilt about being so harsh as I am lucky that they are remembered and certainly left such a huge handprint on the world.

Memories don't work in the way that you might expect them to. When something bad happens, it's hard to accept there can be huge blanks in your recollections and there can be such guilt that, if you've forgotten something, it's because you don't care enough or love enough, or you've moved on. That isn't the case at all. You can have doubts, you can question your reactions and those memory gaps, but you still loved. You really did.

Even now, I'm not scared of dying but I'm scared for Elizabeth once I go. I'm already imagining what it will be like for her when I go. Obviously, she's getting older and her personality is developing but, while she's an absolute whirlwind, she will have this loss in her life forever and who knows what that will do to her? I have to be here for her as long as I can but sometimes it's hard, it's achingly hard and there's always a reminder.

I have to take Stu's death certificate with me when I travel with my daughter. Going into the States on one trip, I was asked where he was.

'He's dead,' I snapped to the woman. If she felt bad with my answer, then I'm afraid she deserved it. For once, I didn't feel bad for someone else.

I can't get away.

It's always with me.

Chapter Twenty-Seven

Looking Forward

I live and breathe *Believe*.

Any time I think I'll get out, even just a little bit, it draws me back in. It is my future. I work for it pretty much full-time but I don't take a penny out. The process of writing this book has made me realise that my life is never going to be normal as such (what is normal anyway?). I have accepted that my life is now very different. It's on a different path to the one I was expecting and hoping for. Everything we do in life leads us to another chapter. With that in mind, we all need to look forward, not back, but that is hard when what you had was so wonderful.

The funny thing is, when I do talks or events, I sometimes feel guilty that Stu isn't the one doing them as he would have loved it! He would have been in his element at The Pride of Britain Awards. The harsh reality is, I'm doing all these things because something immensely painful has happened; I'm not enjoying myself. No one has ever said anything negative to my face, but who knows what some may be thinking behind my back? I have had comments to suggest I step back from *Believe*, to focus on Elizabeth, but that shows how little people understand.

Looking forward, Elizabeth will always be my priority; she will always come first, but I have to do this charity work as well. That doesn't stop me feeling like I'm being stabbed in the heart almost every day. I shut down, put up with it, and carry on with the charity.

But it hurts.

I just want to be back there with my boys but I can't turn back time. It can feel like I'm pushing things uphill all the time. People don't understand how hard it is to run a charity. They think I just pop in and send a few teddy bears out while a team of people support me because we've achieved so much. That couldn't be further from the truth.

As we head into the future without them, Facebook memories will never stop hitting me like a wrecking ball. I watch and re-watch videos of Stu and Fraser and the truth is, it feels good to weep, to bawl, to actually grieve when I do. I just go to my bed and immerse myself in them, crying my heart out and needing them so much. It hurts. Everything hurts. Often it's the lead up or the days following anniversaries that are harder than the actual date. Strangely, it's never the actual day for me.

And then there are my daily internal battles. Every time Zach puts his children back on the train to go to their mum, I know that he misses them so much. But then I feel such a terrible person for thinking, *I don't have that, I'll never see my child again, it'll be forever, not three weeks.* That makes me feel such a bad wife and stepmother – why shouldn't they be upset, why shouldn't they be entitled to their perfectly natural emotions? Nothing is straightforward.

Another aspect that people get wary about is that they don't think they can grieve in the way they want to because my grief is bigger. I know people get upset because their child has gone to university, or they miss them if they're not there on their birthday, I know they do. I try to remember to message them and acknowledge it because I'm so scared that they might think I'm a bad person and I also don't want anyone to feel my pain, but I'm in bits; I'm ripped raw.

When I open up to Zach, he shuts down and can't deal with me being emotional. I've done so well at building up my wall that when it sometimes cracks, he can't feel my pain. How can he? Who would want to think about losing their child?

I ache.

I long for Fraser. I just want to hug him – I hug my bear so many nights, all night long, but it's not him, is it? It's not my baby. It never will be. The waves of grief are terrifying. I could drown. I know I could, and going forward it's the little things that can break me. The little things that most people wouldn't even have to consider.

I bought a new car recently and that was a big deal because I'm still scared of driving. It didn't take long before I had to ask about safety features and I know I emphasised it so much that the salesman was wondering why I was obsessed.

And then my story comes out, it always comes out. I had to tell him why I have to know about safety features in cars, I have to try and justify it. It's like a script but it has changed to protect Zach now. It's changed from pouring out, 'I lost my husband and my son in a road traffic incident in 2015, and therefore I have PTSD but my son did go on to donate his organs which saved four lives,' making it easier for the person to give a positive spin about Fraser.

I'd go on: 'Then I set up a charity to educate and support people about organ donation.' That means they don't have to think about the initial thing. I'd say it to help protect them from feeling uncomfortable.

Nowadays, my parlance is different:

'My daughter lost her brother and her dad in a road traffic incident.' I do it to protect Zach but there's a personal cost to that. The person listening might think I was Stu's second wife, and Fraser's step-mum, but I do it anyway. I feel I'd be doing the boys a disservice if I didn't give something in their memory to make that person know how incredible they were but I do acknowledge that it provides the other person with a get out.

It's all thought out. If I stopped at, 'I lost my husband and my son in a road traffic incident in 2015, and therefore I have PTSD,' they would say, 'I'm sorry for your loss.' But they're not sorry for my loss though, are they? They don't know me; it's just a filler.

Why would you be sorry for my loss? You're just selling me a car, that's a really trite thing to say. You don't have to apologise for my loss, you didn't do anything to cause it. By giving them the second part, I can avoid them saying those things – they can just offer to take a collecting tin for the charity.

The little things that most people wouldn't even have to consider.

All our futures are unknown, but I'm so scared of losing somebody else again and having to cope with all of this on my own. I'm so scared that I'll suddenly become too much for Zach, that I'm not kind enough, I'm not brave enough. I can't risk being alone again, I just can't. It's not that Zach has replaced Stu in my heart – I don't want anyone to think he has – but I want Zach to know that it's different. My heart has grown for him, it really has, but no one can replace someone you lose. I have got happiness again, a different happiness, and I don't want Zach to feel bad about any of this.

I've had to look back to produce this book. Writing all of this down has been unbearable at times as I revisit absolutely everything, but I know it's something I've had to do. The grief at the beginning was a numbness, in fact, for years, I was numb to it all and I would try and distract myself constantly. I always wanted to run things past Stu at the start. It was so strange not to have anybody to check in with, to make decisions with. We were so used to discussing things together and making choices together, and when I didn't have someone to have my back, I was adrift. I felt whatever I did wasn't good enough to please everybody. I didn't realise the most important people to please were me and Elizabeth.

At the time, I didn't grieve in public, I carried out acting my life in the way I deemed was the proper way, the way that wouldn't upset other people. I had to be something acceptable to other people or they would get fed up with me and I'd have no one. I've never really opened up to others and now that window of opportunity has gone. I'm getting there and that's why I'm feeling so much pain and hurt. I am letting that wall down a bit. I was performing for so long, I was the Anna-Louise who was coping, the Anna-Louise who could turn her trauma into something good, who could channel it, and all of that made it easier for other people. Years down the line, they can look at what I've achieved rather than ask what they can do for me, but looking ahead, I still need help. I really do.

If I could ask for anything from other people, it would be that they just hug me. I don't need the words. I don't want any of that on Mothering Sunday or Christmas or their birthdays or the anniversary or any of the 'significant' days when other people celebrate and they suddenly remember I exist. I want to be checked in on to see how Anna's doing, not just because it's one of those 'big days' and they feel obliged.

When people talk about Fraser and Stu, they talk about how they miss them or their children miss their friend. I want them to hear how *I* miss them. I have done everything that I can to try and protect everyone else. It doesn't actually help when someone tells me their child still struggles with Fraser's death or that they still talk about him. It just adds to my pain.

Whenever I do anything charity-wise, people say that they remember where they were when they heard what had happened. That really pisses me off. I know exactly where I was and I can't tell anybody what I saw that night. I've tried through writing this, but I don't think I could ever do it in real life. I couldn't inflict that pain onto another person; I couldn't do it. If anybody saw and understood the pain of what I go through, it would break me.

I also hate the way people say they could never have coped. I don't want any of that 'you've been so brave' response because I just don't see it that way. Maybe being more emotional would have been braver actually, if I'd shown my pain. The way I am absolves them. If I'm brave and they're still struggling, they don't have to do anything because I'm coping.

But I'm not coping. I'm really not.

We're very bad at dealing with loss in our society but if there is one thing to bear in mind, it's don't assume someone else's grief. I could always say that because of Stu – it used to really bug me that he did that. He would feel that he'd known someone better than he had, or he'd been affected so much by someone dying. I'd say, 'Stu, you barely knew them! You'd have struggled to pick them out of a line-up.' He would buy flowers, he'd get upset, and it frustrated me so much. I see other people doing that with him now. I got cross at him so I can feel I can get cross at people who do it to me, I'm not being hypocritical. The fact is, sometimes you don't have to do or say anything, you just have to be there.

A friend of mine who I wasn't that close to at the time got it right and still does. She sends messages that just say, *Thinking of you.* That's the way to do it. Don't force your grief on people, don't ask them questions that they might not want to answer, don't force them into replying, don't grab someone else's grief for yourself – just check. What hurts me is when other friends have major losses, I'm the one who gets the telephone call to ask how they should be dealt with, what should be said. Well, I'm the expert, aren't I? They're not still wondering how I'm doing, are they? I still give the advice, I still give the help, but I'm hurting myself. I do the checking in, I do the making sure everyone is OK, but it's not reciprocated.

Grief doesn't really end. 'Moving on' is a myth – others can do it, but the ones who are at the raging, fiery heart of it? No, that's not an option we have. Does anyone want to listen to what it's really like?

Do you?

I'm not sure because we'll all face it in one way or another, some want to prepare for it, some want to live in denial. But this is my truth, this is my existence, and looking forward, this is what I live with.

And I've finally accepted that I deserve to be heard.

Chapter Twenty-Eight

A Reflection

She Will Be Loved

Stu always used to say to me, 'The race is long, but only with yourself.' I'm constantly comparing myself with other people and how they cope, and I feel I'm failing in every single way. Stu was right - it is a very long race. But I can't find the compassion within myself to say, 'It's not your fault.' I can't grasp those words or find a way to say them to myself.

Everything I've achieved feels like it's just happened; that it wasn't caused by me. If everything goes wrong, that's my fault. That leads to a constant need for validation. I have to know that I'm doing OK because I'm my own worst critic.

What I'm worried about is how I feel about myself. My faith has remained very much a constant. I'm still not scared of dying and I don't think many people can say that. Living is so much harder. Sometimes I wonder what a perfect day would be like if I could magic one up, and I truly think it would be one of reassurance.

I'd love to have one conversation with Fraser and he would say I was a great mum and I made him feel loved. He would tell me he was proud that I had carried on and kept showing love for him. I want him to be proud of what I've done and how I've been mum to Elizabeth.

Stu used to say to me, 'Good morning, Mrs Bates. I love you with all my heart, you truly are my Mrs Wonderful and every day that I wake up with you is more special than the last.' I want to hear that again. I want to know that I am still that special and I'm still being given that love. I want to know that I haven't failed. That, to me, is what I want. When people don't show their support or come to events, the reason I take it so personally is that lack of support is a lack of validation that I'm doing OK. I know my parents are proud of me, but I want it from Stu and Fraser. I want that so much.

Zach is incredible. He is dealing with someone who didn't divorce; he is dealing with someone who loved her husband with all her heart. He knows that I need the validation; I ask him if he still loves me all the time. I have compared my love for them both. I'm only human and that's a natural thing to do, but they're different loves because I'm a different woman now. Zach does validate me as I have to know that I'm doing OK as his wife, not who I was before. I want to know that Stu is proud of the fact that I have been able to love. My love for Stu never falters, just as it never faltered when

I had Fraser, just as my love for them both never faltered when I had Elizabeth.

Now my love for all of them is strong and never falters despite having Zach in my life. When Father Irving said to me, 'The biggest compliment a widow can give is to love again,' he gave a little bit of that validation with those words.

Rather than saying I will never have a perfect day with my boys again, the crux of it is that circumstances change what your perfect day would look like. I can't say what my perfect day with Fraser would look like because *I've* changed. What I need now is different than when the boys were here. My ideal would obviously be to have those hugs, I would love nothing more than to sing with them all, to play racing and horsey games, to put on a family musical, because that isn't my life now. Ultimately, I would just love to know that, however hard it is for me, that they were happy, that they loved me as much as I loved them. If they could just say they were proud, that would be enough.

I never felt that God had taken them from me, it was never His fault. For a long time, I was so fixed on it being no one's fault because if I questioned it too much, I might think it was our fault. I did wonder if it was my purpose though. Did this happen to me because God thought I was strong enough to deal with it all? God didn't cause their deaths, but once it had happened, He saw that I had the potential to make a difference if I could be strong.

Fraser made it to Bristol to allow his donation to happen. He made it through that night to allow the operation to take place the following day. Was that God? Or am I making excuses so that I don't blame him? I don't know where His power lies but it has to be somewhere, I have to feel that. Stu always said that you should show your faith by the way you live and I know God doesn't need me at Mass every week to know that I have that faith. When Zach was in hospital, I prayed for the first time in years. I prayed that he would come home to me and that God could help me to make that happen. I guess I got that so maybe He is helping me out a bit.

Soon after the boys died, Elizabeth and I would say a prayer every night, asking God to look after Stu and Fraser. Now, I check in on them, asking them for signs that they are proud. I've had robins, rainbows, and butterflies, and they're all there if I look for them. But perhaps I want something remarkable, something that I can't deny or explain away.

Stu made me a mix tape when we first started seeing each other and one of the songs was *She Will Be Loved* by Maroon 5. The lyrics talk about the girl with the broken smile and of how things aren't always butterflies and rainbows, of how goodbye means nothing at all. We both loved that song but it means even more now – there are butterflies and rainbows everywhere, and I am still a little bit broken after all. Does goodbye mean nothing as the song goes? No, it means far too much – all I can do is look for those signs.

I have constant doubt. On the night Stu died, he told me that he was so proud of my singing and that was all I wanted. That's what I miss. I know he would want me to love Zach, but I can't convince myself to rely on what my head knows, which makes me end up thinking, again, 'How lucky was I that Fraser made it all the way to Bristol? How lucky was I that he had the strength to do that?' I wasn't lucky at all though, was I? I had the worst luck in the world.

What anyone else throws at me is fine, because no one else can hurt me as much as I hurt myself every day. It's self-harm I guess. I beat myself up that I can't even remember what their last words were to me. I had that night of Fraser sticking me to like glue and we were cwtched up for so long, but his last words? Stu's last words? No, I don't know what they were. All I have are the witness statements which said we were all singing. That has to be enough.

And, as time has gone on, I've had to protect myself with Roman; I can't think about it too much. I can deal with the fact that he is poorly and asking myself what I can do – does he need an iPad, would the time pass quicker for him if he had a Nintendo? But I can't think of what will happen when he dies. That's not my grief. He's got Fraser's heart but he's Zoe's boy. I have to separate the two. I'm so glad I donated Fraser's organs and so glad I met him, but I can't steam in there and appropriate the grief as I know all too well how that feels.

I'd love to wallow. I'd love to just curl up in a ball and rest. An ideal moment would be full of me being supported, almost being a child who is being cared for, whose needs are the priority. I want to be enveloped with love by everyone I love, everyone who has a special part in my heart, telling me they are proud of me. I want them to not take any nonsense from me when I tell them I'm not worth it. I want them to be there and to make me feel that I matter.

In October 2022, I had a message from Zoe that Roman wasn't doing too well at all. That night, I had such nightmares and the following day found myself stuck on the number 'seven'. It would soon be seven years until the anniversary, seven years since the donation, seven years since Roman was born. I was in bits and had to try and get it all out by writing this:

***

Seven.
    Seven years with you
    Seven years without you.
    Seven years of white noise
    Seven years of silence.
    Seven years of desperation.
    Seven years of thankfulness.
    Seven years of longing
    Seven years of hope.
    Seven years of memories

Seven years of memories to make.

Seven years of discovery

Seven years of education.

Seven years of loneliness

Seven years of support.

Seven years of split parenthood

Seven years of single motherhood.

Seven years of weeping

Seven years of smiling through the tears.

Seven years of examination

Seven years of discovery.

Seven years of self-deprecation

Seven years of self-discovery.

Seven years of thunderstorms

Seven years of rainbows and butterflies.

Seven years of doubting

Seven years of believing.

Seven years without you

Seven years still with you xx

***

You can't fix any of this, but you carry it and it becomes part of you. Your grief is your own. The idea that it is somehow not conforming to certain patterns is inhumane. There's recent research that suggests that 'prolonged grief disorder' should be considered a pathology and I feel that undermines everyone who is living with this. It's not wrong for it to last however long it lasts. There is no rule book, and nor should there be. We all have a right to grieve. We don't need labels to say it's OK, we don't need to be told by a medical professional that we've come through it or we've been in it for too long. We don't need to be told the only answer is medication or recovery. This is our normal, and we're entitled to it.

Sadness makes other people uncomfortable but we can't change that, although perhaps we need to look at why there is such discomfort around it in the first place, given that it's a natural human state. Not everything broken can be fixed, but maybe that means we should be looking more at what we mean by 'broken', and why we can't sit with that, rather than thinking everyone can be sorted into a brand-new version of them, a them who isn't affected or scarred by what has happened. A them that is acceptable to society.

I still find it hard to accept that there is a world without the boys in it. How can there be? How can they just have been taken from it, leaving that gap? And yet the world turns.

How?

And there are times when I want to roar, I want to howl, but the cliché of life going on is true. I get the shopping in, I run errands, I clean the house, I do the garden. It's all so small and yet it's what we all do, it's what we fill our lives with, and the loss of those we love doesn't change any of that. We need to live, no matter how mundane that may be, in the middle of the biggest thing in the world happening to us. It's beyond cruel.

In the end, life shouldn't be defined by one moment. It's our duty to live it. Life is a gift and you have a responsibility to make the most of yours. My boys have gone. But what I have to remember and hold to my heart is that they were here. I didn't have them for long enough, but I *did* have them.

I had their love. I gave them my love. I laughed with them and held them; I played with them and I cherished them. I had that world with them and I need to hold onto that. Some people never have that love and they never give it.

There was Stu and there was Fraser.

There is Elizabeth and there is me.

And sometimes that's enough. I just hope that one day, I'll get more of those 'sometimes'. I'll never forget and I'll never not miss them.

But they were here.

They were here and that has to be enough.

Chapter Twenty-Nine

Epilogue

To My Boys

Dearest Stuey,

As I sit here on a cruise ship in the Med and await departure, there is a phrase ringing in my ears – I'm waiting for them to announce that it's 'time to say goodbye'.

And it hits me.

Goodbye again.

That's just it, isn't it? We never had time to say goodbye; we never had time for those words. The truth is, I've avoided even saying it in my heart because it's so painful. I never want to say goodbye to you. I never want to have to face that. How can I deal with really, truly knowing that you're not ever returning? That you and our Fraser Bear remain in another world that I can only hope holds a place for me too one day?

I'm so very sorry I couldn't say goodbye at the time, that I couldn't hold your hand at the road, that I couldn't say a proper goodbye at the hospital. My heart breaks with regret that I didn't say a private goodbye to you in any way.

It's taken me more than six years to get to this point, to feel that I am able to say goodbye. I just hope you can hear me say it and I hope that you are watching everything I'm trying to do with Elizabeth, to make you proud. I never stop telling her what an amazing person you are and what wonderful values you passed onto her. I try to impress upon our little girl how important it is to appreciate the gift of life, and to love each day for you and with you.

Not a day goes by that we don't talk about you, that we don't miss you and cry for you. Our lives may have opened a new chapter but without your unconditional and unfaltering love, we could not, and would not, be able to continue to love.

But it's been so long.

The thing I feel most guilty about is that I feel jealous - jealous that you have Bear. I'm jealous that you don't have to be here, hiding your emotions and dealing with pain. However, I know deep down that you would do anything to help me through this and can only take comfort in the belief that feeling so much pain must mean that what we had was real.

By telling the story of us, I hope I've done you proud, Stuey. I really want you to be looking down and smiling, remembering what we did together and shining with pride at the two wonderful children we made. However, I also know that by writing this, by saying goodbye in these pages, I'm opening myself up to even more pain and hurt. If I finally accept that you've gone, if I allow that word to relate to *you,* then I can't use it as a shield any longer. I know I have to though. I know it's time.

Goodbye my love – and thank you for everything.

Goodbye My Mr Wonderful xxxx

My Fraser Bear,

My gorgeous, fabulous boy. I truly hope you know that you are loved beyond belief and missed beyond measure. I don't have the words to show to you the gap you have left. I can't begin to explain how much I yearn for you. The pain stabs my heart and I feel as if it has settled in my bones, making you a part of me forever.

I'm writing this at the side of a pool, with happy families laughing and shouting, their smiles lighting up their faces, their happiness spilling from them as they simply enjoy life. And I weep.

I write to you and I weep. I couldn't stop these tears no matter how much I tried – and I'm not even sure that I would want to. If I cry for you, I feel for you. I'm scared that if I didn't, I'd lose a part of what you were and who you are.

I can't help but imagine the boy you would have been. What would life have been like for you? Would you know what career you wanted? Would you have still been singing, playing sports, charming everyone with your kindness? You made such an impression in those seven short years, on me and everyone who knew you – but more years have passed, and I can't believe I have been without you as long as I had with you. From the moment you were born, you showed me that my heart could grow, that hearts can *always* grow to accommodate love and you've continued to do that, touching millions of people with your gift.

You will always be my oldest boy, my bear, and as I continue to hug my Fraser *Believe* bear, I recall those last hugs at the party, that night at the party where you spent so much of it at my side.

I'm sorry I couldn't stop any of it, sorry I couldn't change anything, sorry it couldn't have been me instead of you, sorry I failed to protect you my darling, darling boy. You were so brave and managed to survive so long, against all odds to give me some purpose and something positive to focus on. I hope you didn't feel any pain, Fraser, and I hope that if you can see me in pain, you know that I try to hide it and protect your Elizabeth the way you always did. You had the biggest heart and you still do, you will always be my superhero and the fact that you have touched so many people makes me burst with pride.

What I wouldn't do for five more minutes with you, five more hugs with you. Instead, I'm left with the awareness that I'll spend a lifetime without them, a lifetime without you. My baby boy – you showed me that my heart could grow, that a piece of your heart will always be with me, and that love doesn't fade or disappear. It only intensifies, it only deepens, it only finds ways to show itself every day in even the smallest of things.

I will love you forever xxxx

About The Author

Anna-Louise is a renowned advocate, speaker, and campaigner in the fields of organ donation and public health.

Anna-Louise initially had a successful career in law before a personal tragedy led her to found Believe Organ Donor Support. Her career since then has spanned media appearances, award-winning initiatives, and impactful consultations.

Her extensive awards include the ITV People's Campaigner of the Year 2016 and the Pride of Britain Welsh Fundraiser of the Year 2016. Her media engagements include documentaries and appearances on ITV's This Morning and ITV News, in addition to radio.

A prolific public speaker, Anna-Louise has addressed numerous leading businesses and institutions on organ donation, grief, and trauma, and has consulted with leading organisations and governmental bodies. Her incredible experience and achievements stand as a testament to her dedication and impact.

Keep up with Anna-Louise's work at
www.annalouise.wales

About Believe The Charity

Believe is a charity established by Anna-Louise Bates in memory of her late husband, Stuart and her son, Fraser (Bear) Bates whose organ and tissue donations went on to save many lives. The charity's mission is to educate and help spread the word on organ donation, support those people involved, and break down the taboo around organ donation to get people talking. Anna-Louise remains a proud volunteer and CEO of the charity.

To find out more about how to support Believe, scan the QR code below.

About Organ Donation

To find out more about organ donation in the UK, visit:

www.organdonation.nhs.uk

Join the Organ Donation Register at:

www.organdonation.nhs.uk/register-your-decision

About St Martins Church

To find out more about the music at St Martins Church, scan here:

To support the work of St Martins Church, scan here:

Printed in Great Britain
by Amazon